Racism, the Thorn in the Humanity's Peaceful Coexistence

Racism, the Thorn in the Humanity's Peaceful Coexistence

With special reference to Theological, Tribal, Gendered, and Communication Media Perspectives

Edited by
A. Temjen Jamir

Foreword by
Marnungsang

Clark Centre for Peace Research and Action (CCPRA)
Clark Theological College

&

Christian World Imprints™

CCPRA Publication Series No. 9

First Published in 2017 by

Clark Centre for Peace Research and Action (CCPRA)
Clark Theological College
Aolijen, Mokokchung 798601 / Nagaland
ctcprin@gmail.com
www.ctcnagaland.com
Phone: 09402695009

&

Christian World Imprints™
Christian Publishing & Books from India
H-12 Bali Nagar, New Delhi-110015
info@christianworldimprints.com
www.ChristianWorldImprints.com
Phone: +91 11 25465925

ISBN: 978-93-5148-208-6 (HB)
ISBN: 978-93-5148-209-3 (PB)

Printed in India

Contents

Foreword

The Clark Theological College (CTC) is once again elated to publish another book entitled *Racism, the thorn in the Humanity's Peaceful Coexistence*, through the Clark Centre for Peace Research and Action (CCPRA), which is a very unique wing in the ministry of CTC. Since its inception in 2009, CCPRA has been actively involved in the promotion of peace that continues to strengthen the vision and mission of Clark Theological College. The activities undertaken by the CCPRA are aimed at promoting peace by addressing various issues and these are advocated and delivered through peace tours, peace festivals, story/essay writing competitions, consultations, seminars and publications. In addition to this, the Peace Centre Library contains a collection of over 1,000 books which serves thousands of research scholars from across the region for their research works in relation to peace and violence. A joy it is for me to note and assert that the works of the CCPRA are appreciated and strongly supported by the churches and the society at large. Special mention has to be made that the success of the CCPRA is due to the generous contribution and support extended by the EMW, Germany. We are privileged to have such a stronghold body ever willing to extend all the needed support towards the ministry of CTC and CCPRA in particular.

I am delighted to also inform the readers that the CCPRA has already published 9 books addressing the ongoing issues in relation to Peace and Violence. The present volume is the outcome of the two days national seminar organized by the CCPRA from November 5-6, 2015. I thank Ms. C. Pursenla Ozukum, Programme Coordinator, CCPRA for her dedication in making all the yearly projects a success. I appreciate and thank Rev. Dr. A. Temjen Jamir, who has edited this volume. I am also grateful to the Christian World Imprints, New Delhi, for publishing our books.

May all the readers of this book be richly blessed!

Rev. Dr. Marnungsang
Principal
Clark Theological College

Acknowledgement

First of all, I take this opportunity to thank the members of the CCPRA Committee for entrusting me to edit this book for publishing through Christian World Imprints (CWI). In this connection, I would like to express my appreciation to Rev. Dr. Marnungsang, Principal, for giving words of encouragement, advice and support towards the publication of this book.

Special thanks must go to Ms. C. Pursenla Ozukum, Programme Coordinator of CCPRA for taking the initiatives in organizing and conducting the seminar on the theme: *Racism: The Thorn in the Humanity's Coexistence.* She has taken a lot of pain in making all the articles and needed resources available for publication.

All the contributors of the articles in this book deserved our appreciation for giving their time and the best efforts being put into the articles, and also revising them for publication. Without their invaluable contributions the publication of this book could not have been possible.

I would like to express a big thanks to all the staff members of the Christian World Imprints, New Delhi, for extending all the technical help and support. Special thanks must go to Mr. Sudhanshu Kanda, CMO, for providing all the required information and advice for making this publication possible. Ultimately, we want to give glory and honour to our Almighty God for providing all the needs and making this publication a grand success.

Editor

Introduction

This book is a collection of articles presented by scholars during the National Seminar on the theme: ***Racism, the Thorn in Humanity's Coexistence*** organized by Clark Centre for Peace Research and Action (CCPRA) Clark Theological College, Aolijen, Mokokchung, on 5th - 6th November, 2015. Racism can be seen as a deep-seated evil in the society that benefits only some section or dominant group of people in the society, and discriminates the minority and weaker sections of the society without any compassion. It rather encourages division and hatred among the people, thereby, disturbs peaceful co-existence with one another in the society, thus, the book was named, ***Racism, the Thorn in Humanity's Peaceful Coexistence.*** Samuel George's Keynote address highlighted the pertinent issues and concerns of the evil of racism being faced by the people in India, especially people of North East India.

The first chapter deals with some biblical thoughts and views on racism from the Old Testament Pentateuch account by Temsuyanger. In the second chapter, Syiemlieh, uses the key term *ethnocentrism* based on Romans 1:14 and 16, indicating that these references are socio-cultural markers, which can disclose Paul's response to ethnocentric behaviour and attitudes inherent in society.

In the third chapter, Hukato N. Shohe deals with the racism from the tribal custom and practices with special reference to Nagas. In this regard, he points out that in the traditional society, socio-economic, cultural and political discriminations were not practiced among the people due to had given a strong emphasis on communitarian spirit and values in the community. However, in contemporary tribal society, discrimination is being escalated due to scarcity of resources and self interest motives in the society. In the fourth chapter, Shimreingam discusses on racism and Religion (Christianity) from an ethical perspective indicating that racism devalues the culture and lives of racial minorities, and also deprives the opportunity of the racial minorities. It demands our affirmation to overcome such racial discriminations in order to achieve racial equality in the society.

The fifth chapter by Eyingbeni Hümtsoe focuses on the importance of celebrating racial diversity in terms of its divine origin in showing how God's plan of promoting racial diversity is being materialized in and through His Son, Jesus Christ. It provides a strong Christological principle so as to frame out an anti-racist approach and engagement, which will be meaningful for Christian community. In the sixth chapter, Temjensosang argues that racism is socially and structurally generated instrument in the hands of dominant group of people in the society that is so much innate in human culture. In the contemporary society, the greatest threat and challenge to all humanity is global terrorism and it is also the creation of racism. In the seventh chapter, Basaiawmoit deals with the Indian legal perspective on racism highlighting Constitutional Provisions against Racism which is well taken. In the eighth chapter, Toshi Aier discusses some roots and practices of racism in Christian history highlighting such as, Colonialism and Racism, Christianity and Anti-Semitism, and Islamophobia and Discrimination against the Arabs. In this connection, he proposes for an ecumenical involvement in combating racism in the society.

In ninth chapter, A. Temjen Jamir envisages that the media are being used by the dominant class of the society for racial discrimination and oppression of the weaker and vulnerable sections of the society that creates only division, tension, hatred and conflicts among the people in the society. At this juncture, he proposes that the media can be used to combat the evil of racism in the society in order to promote and advocate peaceful coexistence with one another in the society. In the tenth chapter, Butesen looks at the evil of racism from a Christian communication perspective and vehemently argues that despite the fact that the purpose of communication has been hijacked and misinterpreted with selfish interests by few in the society to perpetuate division, hatred and conflict among the people, if the very nature and essence of communication is reaffirmed that is to make commonness, communion, oneness, unity, and peaceful coexistence with one another, then, communication can be remained a source of cure for racism in the society.

The eleventh chapter, Achemlu Ezung attempted to explore re-imagining and relooking at the nexus of gender and racism through prophetic communication with a view to unfold and clarify the negative portrayal of women in media, and the discrimination of women in the church and society that can be seen as racial slur. In this connection, the author attempts to bring out some tentative solution to the problem with some prophetic and liberative note. In the last chapter, while examining the perpetuation and menace of racism in the society from a Christian ministerial perspective, Imtimenba calls upon Christians to witness as an inclusive church for a just and humane community.

The articles were written from different perspectives such as, biblical, theological and ethical, historical and legal, gender, tribal, ministerial and mass media that aimed at provoking the thoughts of the readers and giving a wakeup call on the evil and threat of racism in the society. This volume does not intend to give any solution to the problems but appeals everyone to be perceptive and active with a spirit of commonality towards the pain and thorns in many forms that innocent people are made to experience everyday in the most inhuman acts, so that we may be able to give more space for peace and justice in the society.

A. Temjen Jamir

Keynote Address

Samuel George[1]

Locating the Debate

Let me begin with two incidents of racial attacks on people from North-East India, one in the national (international?) capital of Information Technology – Bangalore and the other in the national capital of India – New Delhi.

On April 18, 2012, Richard Loitam, a 19 year old, second-semester student of Acharya NRV School of Architecture, Bangalore was found dead on his hostel bed. While the police initially said he died as a result of a road accident, the student's friends and family alleged he suffered fatal injuries in an assault by seniors a day earlier. The death sparked off protests in Bangalore and New Delhi. There are enough evidences to show that it was a racially motivated attack on a person from North-East of India.

On January 29, 2014, Nido Taniam, a young boy from Arunachal Pradesh was killed for looking 'different.' He was harassed for his hairstyle, and appearance (he was called 'Chinese') and that resulted in a tiff with whom he had asked direction to a friend's

1 Dr. Samuel George is Professor in the Department of Christian Theology at Allahabad Bible Seminary (Senate of Serampore), Uttar Pradesh. He is a member of the Reference Group of EDAN-World Council of Churches. He also serves as the Resident Editor of the *New Life Theological Journal* (ISSN 2455-0027). He has authored the following books: *Christology – An Introduction* (2013); *The Historical Particularity of Jesus: A Dialogue with the Hindu View of History* (2014); *The Gospel as Public Truth: An Indian Multi-Religious Perspective on Lesslie Newbigin* (2014); *Ekklesia: Indian Conversations* (ed. 2015); *Jesus Beyond Borders: Towards a 'Glocal' Christology* (ed. 2016).

house. He was very severely assaulted by seven/eight persons. The next day he was found dead. It was a clear incident of racial attack.

The Concept Paper of the Seminar defines the parameters of the discussion as: "The evil of racism in India with special reference to the people of North East India who have been often at the receiving end of such racial prejudices, exploitation, and discrimination in the main-line India." The focus of the Seminar is the evil of racism in India and more specifically the racial prejudices faced by people of North-East India.

This paper is addressed from a Christian theological (biblical and theological) perspective.

Defining the terms

Race

It is the idea that the human species is divided into distinct groups on the basis of inherited physical and behavioural differences. However, genetic studies in the 20th century refuted the existence of biogenetically distinct races, and scholars now argue that 'races' are cultural interventions reflecting specific attitudes and beliefs that were imposed on different populations in the wake of western European conquests beginning in the 15th century. The idea of 'race' began to evolve in the late 17th century, after the beginning of European exploration and colonization, as a folk ideology about human differences associated with the different populations—Europeans, Amerindians, and Africans—brought together in the New World. In the 19th century, after the abolition of slavery, the ideology fully emerged as a new mechanism of social division and stratification.[2] Over the time, the term race has been applied in different ways: to linguistic groups (the "Arab race" or the "Latin race"), to religious groups (the "Jewish race"), and even to political, national, or ethnic groups with few or no physical traits that distinguish them from their neighbours (the "Irish race," the "French race," the "Spanish race," the "Slavic race," the "Chinese race", etc.).

2 Peter Wade, "Race," *Encyclopedia Britannica Online,* http://www.britannica.com/topic/race-human (accessed October 07, 2015).

Michael James points out that the concept of race has historically signified the division of humanity into a small number of groups based upon five criteria:

1. Races reflect some type of biological foundation, be it Aristotelian essences or modern genes.
2. This biological foundation generates discrete racial groupings, such that all and only all members of one race share a set of biological characteristics that are not shared by members of other races.
3. This biological foundation is inherited from generation to generation, allowing observers to identify an individual's race through her ancestry or genealogy.
4. Genealogical investigation should identify each race's geographic origin, typically in Africa, Europe, Asia, or North and South America.
5. This inherited racial biological foundation manifests itself primarily in physical phenotypes, such as skin colour, eye shape, hair texture, and bone structure, and perhaps also behavioural phenotypes, such as intelligence or delinquency.[3]

Racism

The Oxford Dictionary defines racism as: "Prejudice, discrimination, or antagonism directed against someone of a different race based on the belief that one's own race is superior."

The Apple Dictionary defines racism as "the belief that all members of each race possess characteristics, abilities, or qualities specific to that race, especially so as to distinguish it as inferior or superior to another race or races."

The *Encyclopedia Britannica* defines Racism, also called racialism as, "any action, practice, or belief that reflects the racial worldview—the ideology that humans are divided into separate and exclusive biological entities called 'races,' that there is a causal link

3 Michael James, "Race," *The Stanford Encyclopedia of Philosophy* (Fall 2015 Edition), Edward N. Zalta (ed.), <http://plato.stanford.edu/archives/fall2015/entries/race/> (accessed October 07, 2015).

between inherited physical traits and traits of personality, intellect, morality, and other cultural behavioural features, and that some races are innately superior to others."[4]

The United Nations defines racism as "any distinction, exclusion, restriction or preference based on race, colour, descent, or national or ethnic origin." So, treating people different because they are from a different tribe or ethnic group is racist.

Racism is a "tool to create hatred" that one is superior and the other inferior. The above-mentioned definitions both of race and racism point to the fact that this phenomenon is an enforced opinion, a social construction. I contend that racism is rooted in privilege and power, and when asserted, is meant to create fear and to disempower an individual.

India and Racism

India is one of the most xenophobic countries in the world. This is not an exaggeration. Facts defy the perception that we Indians are a tolerant group of people. **Well, we are not.**

Max Fisher in one of his critical analysis in *The Washington Post* has pointed out that India and Jordan by far are the least tolerant countries in the world. In only two of 81 surveyed countries, more than 40% of respondents said they would not want a neighbour of a different race. This included 43.5% of Indians and 51.4% of Jordanians.[5]

Two perspectives: an 'Outsider's' view (Afro-American) and an 'Insider's' view (North-East India) would substantiate my contention that we Indians are one of the most racist in the world.

Diepiriye Kuku, an Afro-American doctoral research scholar at the Delhi School of Economics writes:

---

4 Audrey Smedley, "Racism," *Encyclopedia Britannica Online*, http://www.britannica.com/topic/racism (accessed October 07, 2015).

5 Max Fisher, "A Fascinating Map of the World's Most and Least Racially Tolerant Countries," *The Washington Post* (May 15, 2013) https://www.washingtonpost.com/blogs/worldviews/wp/2013/05/15/a-...g-map-of-the-worlds-most-and-least-racially-tolerant-countries/ (accessed July 17, 2015).

> Racism in India is systematic and independent of the presence of foreigners of any hue. This climate permits and promotes this lawlessness and disdain for dark skin. Most Indian pop icons have light-damn-near-white skin. Several stars even promote skin-bleaching creams that promise to improve one's popularity and career success. Matrimonial advertisements boast of fair, very fair and very very fair skin alongside foreign visas and advanced university degrees.[6]

Kuku rightly identifies the malice among the Indians: "It is shocking that people wear liberalism as a sign of modernity, yet revert to ultra conservatism when actually faced with difference."[7] He further states that:

> Outside of specific anchors of discourse such as Reservations, there is no consensus that discrimination is a redeemable social ill. This is the real issue with discrimination in India: her own citizens suffer and we are only encouraged to ignore situations that make us all feel powerless. Be it the mute-witnesses seeing racial difference for the first time, kids learning racism from their folks, or the blacks and north-easterners who feel victimised by the public, few operate from a position that believes in change.[8]

For this Afro-American research scholar, living in India was a childhood dream that deepened with his growing understanding of India and America's unique, shared history of non-violent revolution. Yet, for him, in most nations, the path of ending gender, race and class discrimination is unpaved. In India, this path is still rural and rocky as if this nation has not decided the road even worthy. It is a footpath that the racially 'different' are left to tread individually.

6 Diepiriye Kuku, "India Is Racist, And Happy About It. A Black American's first-hand experience of footpath India: No one even wants to change," *Outlook Magazine* (June 29, 2009), http://www.outlookindia.com (accessed October 20, 2015).

7 Ibid.

8 Ibid.

Writing from a North-East India perspective, Jilangamba rightly points out that in India there is an institutionalized form of racism. He writes,

> Quite expectedly, such an assertion about the existence of racism in India will not be taken seriously; the response will be to either remain silent [*or*] refuse to acknowledge this form of racism or, fiercely, to reject it. Ironically, most Indians see racism as a phenomenon that exists in other countries, particularly in the West, and without fail, see themselves as victims. They do not see themselves harbouring (potentially) racist attitudes and behaviour towards others whom they see as inferior.[9]

Let me quote few examples of institutionalized forms of racism: In 2011, the University of Hyderabad chose an 'initiative' to curb drinking and drug use on campus by working with students from the North-East of India. In 2007, the Delhi Police decided to solve the problems of security faced by the North-Easterners in Delhi, particularly women, by coming up with a booklet entitled *Security Tips for North East Students* asking north-eastern women not to wear 'revealing dresses' and gave kitchen tips on preparing bamboo shoot, *akhuni*, and 'other smelly dishes' without "creating ruckus in neighbourhood."

What Kuku and Jilangambahad said makes my position more tenable that Indians are Racist. Let's face it openly. The problem has been that we were and are not willing to openly accept it. Rather very subtly we push it under the carpet. The evil of racism cannot be 'solved' unless we accept that there is a problem with us.

North-East 'Indians' as victims of Racism

Every year thousands of people move from North-East of India to other parts of India in search of education, jobs, medical facilities, and 'better' life. Soon, for many, the new environment becomes a nightmare.

---

9 Yengkhom Jilangamba,"Let's stop pretending there's no racism in India," *The Hindu* (May 29, 2012) http://www.thehindu.com/opinion/op-ed/lets-stop-pretending-theres-no-racism-inindia/article3466554.ece (accessed October 16, 2015).

A recent study conducted by Jamia Millia Islamia's Centre for North East Studies and Policy Research with National Commission for Women found that 60% of women from North-East India, who have moved to major cities in India, faced racial harassments and discrimination. New Delhi was reported to be one of the most racially intolerant and discriminating cities where 81% of women faced racial harassment. Racism is not only limited to intolerance within people; it is also aggravated by governments in the name of official procedure (I have earlier mentioned this aspect as institutionalized racism). Women folks from North-East India continues to face most of the racial brunt in mainline India. While discussing the problems faced by women from North-East India, a former lady-colleague of mine told me,

> Racist perceptions often cast us as anti-national, backward and immoral. This effect North-East Indian men and women in different ways. In many instances, North-East Indian women are cast as loose in morals and sexually promiscuous. Such stereotypes feed discrimination on many grounds: workplaces, housing etc. The stereotyping of the immoral Northeasterner is used by many landlords and housing agents to justify higher rents.

The experience of racism faced by the North-East Indians is of a different order. Anant Mishra (a journalist with special interest in North-East India) writes, "It is much more 'in your face,' because of their different racial appearance, different ethnicity (skin colour and looks, language, cultural indifferences and difficulty in pronouncing names)."[10] Every moment of their life outside the boundaries of North-East India they have to beg to be accepted as 'Indians.' The act of racism and violence against North-East Indians are not new. They are targeted everywhere irrespective of their work, their location. The main reason that drives this insane mentality is how they 'look different' from others and their distinct cultures and traditions. Often they are victims of racial slurs that are hurled at them. They are called: '*chinki,*' '*chowmein,*' '*Chinese,*' '*Nepalese.*' Is this

10 http://www.newswithchai.in/2015/04/21/India-divided-racism-attacks-on-north-east-Indian-citizens/ (accessed October 24, 2015).

racial approach towards North-East 'Indians' due to ignorance of the social communities in mainline India? Well, that notion is partly 'correct' but not the whole truth. The distant cultures and traditions of North-East 'Indians' are seen as 'different' therefore, a threat to their community.

There is yet another, subtle and dangerous reason for this discrimination against North-East India. The exclusive Brahmanical imagination of a Hindu *Rashtra* (Hindu majoritarianism) has resulted in ignoring, alienating and subordinating the numerous 'Others' including the tribal communities of North-East India. They are the 'Other' therefore, 'different.' They need to prove their Indianness by 'adjusting' and conforming to the norms and ideals of the majority. Unfortunately, in the case of people from North-East India this racial 'Otherness' is considered as backward or tribal and the 'difference' as 'inferior.' Unless these graded inequalities of 'Othering the Other' are confronted, and challenged both at individual and corporate levels, they will continue to fan venom of racism.

Racism and Religion

The issue of race cannot be understood adequately without getting to know its relation with religion. This is a religious gathering and probably all of us are religious in some sense. Therefore, it is crucial that we discuss the evil of racism from a religious point of view.

Race and religion are intertwined. Centre for Psychology of Religion at Leuven[11] has come out with a startling revelation that there are enough empirical evidences to show that religion is associated with increased prejudice, ethnocentrism and racism,[12] rather than

---

11 Cf. B. Duriez and D. Hutsebaut, "The Relation Between Religion and Racism: the Role of Post-Critical Beliefs," *Mental Health, Religion & Culture* 3, no. 1 (2000): 85-102; B. Duriez, D. Hutsebaut, and F. Roggen, "Racism and Post Critical Belief: A New Approach to an Old Problem," *Journal of Empirical Theology* 12, no. 1 (1999): 5-27.

12 It should be noted here that people who do not deal with religion as a way of life, and who have a closed attitude of external critique too are vulnerable to racism. These are people who have a very simplistic, very confident form of unbelief, based on slogans and elementary reasonings. It can also take the form of a superficial, egocentric approach to life based only on consumption,

with increased love and tolerance.[13] For a Christian theologian (anywhere) this is a source of uneasiness and a true challenge. The Leuven psychologists conclude that religiousity of a person cannot automatically indicate anything about h-er/is ethnocentrism or racism. However, the presence or absence of racism depends on the way in which the person experiences h-er/is religious involvement.[14] A theology that is concerned with humanity (it ought to be) finds here a criterion for critically examining concrete religiousity. Pollefeyt writes:

> Both orthodoxy and externally critical persons [refer the conclusions of Leuven psychologist, cf. footnote no. 12] long for certainty, experience feelings of anxiety and anomy, and have difficulty with symbolic thinking. Historical relativists, on the other hand, refer to their relation to the absolute as a searching process in which there is room for doubt and for a constant renewal of perspectives and complementary interpretations of (religious) reality. I will argue that the main religious viewpoint of orthodox and external-critical persons is characterized by 'closedness,' and that of historical relativists by 'openness.'[15]

It is often noted that to escape the conflicts and unsolvable ambivalences of life, people tend to withdraw from complex and broken reality, taking refuge in safe and unquestionable politico-religious constellation of unchangeable truths that gives foundation

---

or extreme nationalism. Cf. Didier Pollefeyt, "Racism and Christian Belief: A Theological Reflection," *Journal of Empirical Theology* 12, no. 1 (1999): 32.

13 Four important conclusions of the research are: 1). Racism is clearly influenced by religious orthodoxy, which in turn mainly influenced by religiousity as a way of life, and which also seems to be a possible outlook (though to a lesser degree), when religiousity is seen as not so important; 2). Racism is also influenced, but to a lesser degree, by an attitude of external critique towards religion, which is in turn influenced by religiousity as of secondary importance in life; 3). Historical awareness in religious belief (not relativism) is not related to racism, and is itself strongly influenced by religiousity as a way of life; 4). Not considering religion important seems to preclude a historically aware approach to religion. Cf. Ibid., 28-29.

14 Ibid.

15 Ibid., 29.

to their anxious existence (both individual and collective). In such a scenario truth (religious or otherwise), is not the result of a dynamic process of critical and patient enquiry, of questioning and wrestling with the divine, but is generated by the closed, internally coherent logic of the pre-established viewpoint. Here, religion becomes the secure answer to all human questions. In this position, fear of existential meaninglessness hides behind the illusion of absolute religious (or a religious) certainties. Such inflexible religious (or a religious) views will try to neutralize every difference and will stand in opposition to openness, receptivity and vulnerability to real alterity (otherness).[16] In other words, closed stories will try to subsume everything in the circle of sameness. In such an attitude, the greatest danger and crime is 'difference.' Everything that is not assimilable becomes an eminent threat to the beautiful and internally coherent story, and must therefore be excluded and even be exterminated (cf. extermination of minorities in Nazi Germany). Racism, in this sense, is a logical outcome of such an attitude.[17] Everything that cannot or will not integrate into the smooth harmony and dares to endanger the unruffled unity must be dealt with contempt (cf. Hindutva ideology). For someone who objectifies such a worldview, the stranger does not represent a challenge for growth and possible enrichment, indeed a way to God, but will only be experienced as a terrifying invader who must be converted, neutralized or eliminated.

Explaining further Pollefeyt writes,

> A religious position oriented towards existential 'hyperstability' will often be based on some all-regulating internal or external prescriptions that have to be strictly and scrupulously followed, with violation leading to merciless sanctions. This attitude does not believe in humans as beings who are able to understand truth and falsehood, good and evil, on the basis of a formed conscience. When people in such a situation discover the stranger, the non-assimilable within themselves, they will be forced to darken these intrapsychic or social enormities anxiously, for both others and themselves. In this position of

16 Ibid., 30.

17 Ibid.

anxious closedness, racist scapegoating and hypocrisy will go hand in hand.[18]

Orthodoxy and externally critical belief are clearly related to racism. Interestingly, orthodoxy shows a higher correlation to racism than does externally critical belief. It is so because orthodoxy relies heavily on a system, an institution that externalizes and so strengthens closedness in objective structures, rules, hierarchies, etc., whereas an externally critical believer relies on h-er/is own norms and attitudes, and so h-er/is closedness is not necessary doubled by a closed external system. In this way, it can be assumed that religious (orthodox) belief renders the closed system more absolute (divinisation) than it does in the context of non-belief (external critique).[19] Anthropology plays an important role in this interplay of racism and religiousity.[20] Human beings have a certain way of experiencing religion based on their basic *human* condition of openness or closedness. Moreover, religiousity as a way of life correlates mostly with orthodoxy can be read as an indication that people very often experience religion first and foremost as a way of life that offers certainty. It is in this sense one can deduce that religion can induce racism.

However, a religiousity accompanied by historical awareness will lead to openness. And this can stem the tide of racism. Such a religiousity is experienced here as a never-ending process that is always open towards the future, rather than as a final goal which has to be conquered as soon as possible (as is the case with orthodoxy). Here, every question leads to a new insight that in turn raises new questions. It is therefore, in such religiousity symbolism and metaphors becomes important part of its day-to-day affairs. The only 'fixed' point for such believers is the dynamic, free movement of the search for religious truth itself. Religion for them is not the answer to all human questions, but the question mark placed after all

18 Ibid., 30-31.

19 Ibid., 31.

20 For a good reference on anthropology and racism refer to Gary W. Deddo, "Neighbors in Racial Reconciliation: The Contribution of a Trinitarian Theological Anthropology," *Cultural Encounters* 3, no. 2 (2007): 27-46.

our easy, superfluous or egocentric answers.[21] Religion in this sense is not to give certainty, but to question all the certainties the world promises to people. Seen from this perspective, God, then, is not the ultimate guarantee of the ruling, established order, but the One who comes in the face of the **Other**, especially the **stranger**, as a challenge and an opportunity, because God questions the self-righteousness of individual and collective existence.[22]

Racism: Biblical and Theological Reflections

Often, the Bible and its messages are seen from an ethnocentric reality. However, a serious study of the Bible puts a question mark on such interpretations.

There's a common perception that the God of the Old Testament, is out of touch with the issues of race.[23] One may ask, why do people think that Yahweh is racist? Two reasons can be deduced: first, nineteenth-century Christians used Old Testament texts to support slavery based on race, which could suggest that God of the Old Testament tolerates discrimination. Second, Yahweh commanded the Israelites to kill all the Canaanites, which sounds like a divine mandate for genocide.[24]

"In the beginning" of the Old Testament, in Genesis, one finds the foundation laid down for a biblical understanding of race. God created humanity: man and woman in the image of God and then commanded them to multiply and fill the earth (Gen. 1:26-28). Over time humanity grew into numerous groups of peoples, nations,

---

21 Pollefeyt, "Racism and Christian Belief: A Theological Reflection."

22 Ibid.

23 Cf. William R. Jones, *Is God a White Racist? A Preamble to Black Theology* (Boston: Beacon Press, 1998). British pop singer Lily Allen asks in her 2009 single 'Him' about God, "Do you think his favourite type of human is Caucasian?" Dawkins writes, "The God of the Old Testament is arguably the most unpleasant character in all fiction: jealous and proud of it; a petty, unjust, unforgiving control-freak; a vindictive, bloodthirsty ethnic cleanser; a misogynistic, homophobic, racist, infanticidal, genocidal, filicidal, pestilential, megalomaniacal, sadomasochistic, capriciously malevolent bully." Richard Dawkins, *The God Delusion* (London: Bantam Press, 2006), 31.

24 David T. Lamb, *God Behaving Badly: Is the God of the Old Testament Angry, Sexist, and Racist?* (Downers Grove, Illinois: IVP, 2011), 71-72.

clans, tribes, all of which reflect the divine image. Any attitude that denigrates people on the basis of race is, therefore, not only racist but also insulting to the God in whose image they are created. Racism, therefore, is blasphemous, because Bible, in an unequivocal sense informs us that the people of each and every ethnicity resemble God himself. Genesis story is the story of the human family; accordingly all nations are ultimately related to each other. Racism, therefore, is not only insulting to God, but is also insulting to our extended family – the human family.

The Law mandated the Israelites to treat foreigners just like other Israelites (Lev. 24:22; Num. 9:14; 15:15-16). Moses clearly mentioned that God is not racist:

> For the Lord your God is God of gods and Lord of lords, the great, the mighty, and the awesome, who is not partial and takes no bribe, who executes justice for the orphan and the widow, and who loves the **strangers**, providing them food and clothing. You shall also love the **strangers**, for you were **strangers** in the land of Egypt.[25]

The inclusion of the stories of Ruth (a Moabite),[26] Naaman (2 Kgs. 5:1-4, 9-15), Nebuchadnezzar, Darius (Daniel), Ninevehites (Jonah) in the Bible suggest that the authors of the Old Testament wanted to emphasize that God welcomes, heals and loves **foreigners**.

There are numerous instances in the Old Testament that talk about the inclusive nature of God's plan for humanity.[27] In Amos 9:7 God says to the 'people of God,' "Are you not like the Ethiopians to me, O people of Israel? says the Lord. Did I not bring Israel up from the land of Egypt, and the Philistines from Caphtor and the Arameans from Kir?" God had a special relationship with Israel (Amos 3:2), however, they could claim no special favour based upon

25 Deut. 10:17-19 (*NRSV*).

26 Cf. Moab was born out of an incest relationship between a father and daughter (Gen. 19). As per the Mosaic Law they are not to be allowed in the assembly of the Lord (Deut. 23:3).

27 Cf. Ex. 22:20-24; 23:9; Lev. 19:33; Deut. 23:7; 24:14; 27:19: Ezek. 22:7, 29; Zech. 7:10; Mal. 3:5; Ps. 146:9.

their past experience of the Exodus, for God had performed the same feat for the Philistines and Arameans. Nor could they boast of their present wealth for God was doing the very same thing for the Kushites/Ethiopians. In the wider scope of Amos' theology, God is not just the one who cares for Israel. God is a universal sovereign, guiding and directing the histories and destinies of all nations.[28] The Kushites are mentioned in Amos 9:7a, as an example of God's freedom and prerogative to act favourably and beneficently on behalf of all the people of the earth.

The 'foreign' grandmothers of Jesus (**Tamar** - Canaanite, **Rahab** - Canaanite, **Ruth** - Moabite, **wife of Uriah** - Hittite) (Mt. 1:1-6), demolishes the myth of racial purity of the Davidic dynasty. Rather, the foreign ancestry of Jesus highlights so clearly the inclusive nature of 'God's people.'

Jesus was a xenophile.[29] His messages/parables and ministry were littered with examples of foreigners and his interactions with them: a widow cared for by Elijah and Namaan the Syrian (Lk. 4); his interaction with the Samaritan woman (John 4); healing of the daughter of the Syrophoenician woman (Mk. 7); he was furious that foreigners (nations) were not allowed to pray in the temple (Mk. 11). The parable of the 'Good Samaritan' (Lk. 10:29-37) is primarily a story about racism. For Jesus, racism could be over come only with compassion. The compassion of the Samaritan led him to acts of extreme hospitality towards someone who probably would have hated him because he was a foreigner. Jesus told stories combating racism and he actively loved and welcomed foreigners.

The Council at Jerusalem (Acts 15) is a watershed moment in the history of Christianity in terms of its relationship with others. The central issue on the agenda of this first Council was the Church's teaching on race relations. Theologians and historians have often 'neglected' this Council's messages and have spent more energy on deciphering the intricacies of the subsequent Councils of Nicaea,

---

28 Regina Smith, "A New Perspective on Amos 9:7a: 'To Me, O Israel, you are just like the Kushites'," *The Journal of the Interdenominational Theological Center* 22, no. 1 (Fall 1994): 47.

29 Lamb, *God Behaving Badly: Is the God of the Old Testament Angry, Sexist, and Racist?*, 86.

Chalcedon and others. Grand says, "For the New Testament writers it was the race issue that touched the nerve of evangelical Christian faith."[30]

According to the Biblical view of race, there are two groups of men and women: "the people" and "the nations." Lineal descendants of Abraham are the 'chosen' people of God. Interestingly, divisions among "the nations" of the world – Africans, Asians, Europeans, black, yellow, white – have very little significance in the 'plan' of God. The early Christian community (predominantly Jewish) was reluctant to accept Europeans into full fellowship, probably because of the socio-political threat to them by the Europeans who had special position within the Roman Empire. Paul's massive missionary campaign among the Europeans made their push for equality within the people of God the most obvious "race problem" for the Jewish majority in the early Church.[31]

Paul, through his teachings that "… to make everyone see what is the plan of the mystery hidden for ages in God who created all things," (Eph. 3:9) challenges his readers to look to the very inception of divine revelation for confirmation of the truth of this revelation which he now boldly proclaimed. This 'plan' of God is found even in the formation of God's people at the Exodus where "a mixed crowd also went up with them" from Egypt (Ex. 12:38).

It is interesting to note the gradual progression of ethnic identity turning into an ethnocentric identity among the 'people of God.' The most surprising challenge to the ethnocentricity of the Old Covenant came in the Lord's command to prophet Jonah to proclaim judgment against the Ninevehites. To the displeasure of Jonah, these outsiders received mercy as God's children. The oracles of Old Testament prophets are stark reminder of God's 'plan' to include 'the nations' as 'people of God.' However, it remained hidden until proselyting was reformed by the explosive force of Pentecost.[32]

The Holy Spirit forced "the working out of the mystery" on the Church before the issue of inclusion was grasped by the

30 James La Grand, Jr., "The Teaching of the Church on Race Relations," *Reformed Journal* 21, no. 5 (1971): 12.

31 Ibid.

32 Ibid., 13.

Apostles. The deacons became the agents of the early inclusions. Their obedience to the Spirit of Christ broke up the comfortable sectarian life of the Jewish Christians in Jerusalem. It is interesting to note God did not allow the Church to build slowly as legitimate synagogue communities protected by the special tolerance the Jews had won for themselves within the Roman Empire. "If the Twelve had hoped to control the race issue within the established proselyting structures by ordaining deacons for the 'Hellenists,' this hope was soon dashed."[33] It is the inclusion and preaching of the deacons that created the foremost environment of the discussion of race issue in the Early Church.

Racism and the Church

Racism continues to be one of the biggest obstacles to human dignity in the world today. What is the role of the Christian community – the Church in alleviating the evil of racism from the world? Many churches in the West and apartheid South Africa have radically addressed this issue. Some churches have been working diligently not only to challenge diverse forms of discrimination, but have also initiated programs designed to promote greater understanding and acceptance across multicultural and religious lines. But the question remains: has it done enough? Statement from the WCC conference on Racism Today states that: the churches have not done as much as they should in addressing racial and other exclusionary practices within their own ranks. This is a state of affairs, which cannot continue if the churches are to have any credibility in their claim to be the Body of Christ. Because the very nature of racial and other forms of discrimination entails levels of economic, social, and political marginalization which create profound suffering and life-long hardship, our local and national churches cannot continue to ignore this nightmarish reality in which men, women, and children of God are condemned to live. The entire Body of Christ has a prophetic task to denounce by word and deed all forms and expressions of existence, which constrain the reality of the abundant life which God, offered to us in Jesus Christ. Our failure to do so

33 Ibid.

constitutes disobedience to the God we endeavour to serve through faithful discipleship.[34]

Despite the fact that Bible addresses the issue of race repeatedly, the Christian Church doesn't seem to be doing any better than the people in Old Testament or New Testament times. Church, which ought to be an alternative community, lags behind secular institutions including the executive and judiciary.

Coming to the context of India, the issue of race from a church perspective is almost unheard. Churches in India are so divided on Caste, class, ethnic, and tribal lines that the sin of racism do not find mention in its theological and mission agenda.

If the Church in India is to take a radical lead in the pursuance of racial reconciliation, then concerted theological efforts must be exerted toward that end.

Racism and Christian Theology

Traditional theologies often had to do a lot of 'catching up' with the secular world, the reason being its stubbornness in not'discerning the signs of the times.' It has often ignored, neglected and many a times rejected the issues facing the world as subjects of theologizing. Its methods of theologizing which, for a long time, intentionally neglected the material conditions of the very people who professed allegiance to the Christian faith. The theological methods espoused in churches, its related institutions and seminaries fail to equip Christians with tools that are relevant to the context and praxis of the subjugated communities.

A relevant theology should spring from the dynamic of life. It should arise from the deep concern and involvement of simple people both in Christian faith and in the situation of human beings.[35]

34 "Statement from the WCC conference on Racism Today and the Rationale for Continued Ecumenical Engagement, Cleveland, Ohio, 26-29 August 2010," https://www.oikoumene.org/en/resources/documents/wcc-programmes/unity-mission-evangelism-and-spirituality/just-and-inclusive-communities/racism/statement-from-the-wcc-conference-on-racism-today (accessed October 30, 2015).

35 Károly Tóth, "Theology of Liberation and Its Relation to Antiracism," *Communio Viatorum* 18, no. 1-2 (1975): 52.

Experiences of the subjugated communities are to be part of the conversations in theological formation.[36]

Well, it is an open secret that Indian theologies including contextual theologies have not 'adequately' addressed the issue of racism in India. I think Indian churches and its theologies have lagged far behind the secular institutions in addressing this issue. It is important that we address it adequately considering the fact that India is one of the most racist countries in the world. A theology against racism in the Indian context is the need of the hour. Such a theology ought to be contextual, liberational and praxis oriented. Cues are taken from Black theologies in the United State of America and similar liberational theologies elsewhere.[37]

The anti-racist Black theology[38] begins with a critique of traditional theologies, which is basically built on Eurocentric-white male dominated ideologies. Such theologies have generally maintained the status quo and have been identified primarily with the structures of power and only secondarily with the victims of power. In America, the Christian tradition is identified with the structures of racism in their oppression of black people. Cone writes, "This was the reason for the white church's compliance with black slavery, its subsequent indifference to oppression generally, and its

---

36 Rothney Stok Tshaka, "Do Our Theological Methodologies Help us to Deal with Situations of Violence in Black Communities, Specifically Afrophobia?," *Journal of Theology for Southern Africa* 138, (2010): 135.

37 It is 'necessary' for an Indian Christian theology against racism to learn from Black theologies (James H. Cone, Cornel West and others) emerged in the US and the anti-apartheid theologies (Desmond Tutu, Allan Boesak, Beyers Naude, and Frank Chikane) in South Africa. The 'necessity' arises out of two reasons: firstly, no Indian theologies have addressed it; and secondly, there is a similarity of contexts between the United States of America and South Africa and India, i.e., multi-cultural, multi-ethnic contexts where such liberational theologies against racism has emerged.

38 Cf. James H. Cone, *Black Theology and Black Power*, 20th anniversary edition ed. (New York: Harper & Row, 1969; reprint, 1983); James H. Cone, *A Black Theology of Liberation* (Maryknoll, New York: Orbis Books, 1970; reprint, 1993); James H. Cone, *God of the Oppressed*, Revised ed. (Maryknoll, New York: Orbis Books, 1997).

failure to respond to authentic demands of black reparations."[39] Seldom do we find white theologians taking the oppression of black people as a point of departure for analysing the meaning of the Gospel today. Cone opines that white theologians see no connection between blackness and the Gospel of Jesus Christ.[40] The only way it can be done is to take the side of the oppressed. The victims of racial discrimination (in India) are the starting point of the Indian theology against racism. It begins with them. The victims are the "movers and shakers" of this theology.

Since the traditional theologies have neglected and suppressed the marginalized (black) voices in America, it was necessary for the Black theology to look beyond the white Christian tradition to the biblical tradition, investigating the latter in the light of the past and present manifestation of the black struggle for liberation.

Black theology takes very seriously the biblical tradition (both the Old Testament and the New Testament) and the past and present Afro-American revolution. For it the content of Christian theology is liberation. Cone writes, in that sense, "theology is a rational and passionate study of the revolutionary activity of God in the world in the light of the historical situation of an oppressed community, relating the forces of liberation to the essence of the Gospel, which is Jesus Christ."[41] Such a theology moves us in the direction of biblical tradition, which focuses on the activity of God in history, liberating people from human bondage.

As noted earlier under the section **Bible and Racism**, God of the Bible is an inclusive God. 'He' creates all and loves all. 'He' is known by what 'He' does i.e., liberation of the oppressed – 'a preferential option for the poor, marginalized and oppressed.' God's act of liberation in its ultimately form is seen on the Cross at Calvary, where Jesus takes upon himself all human oppression and sin. His death was a public spectacle (victims of racism are often jeered upon. Their human dignity is publically trampled upon).

---

39 James H. Cone, "Christian Theology and the Afro-American Revolution," *Christianity and Crisis* 30, no. 10 (June 1970): 124.

40 Ibid.

41 Ibid., 124.

The resurrection of Jesus is the symbol of God's act of transforming the oppression into transformation. People (oppressed) can now be what they are – liberated humans. To this great mission of "to let the oppressed go free" (Lk. 4:18), God invites us. This is possible only when we lose our identity with the structures that promote, propagate and maintain the status quo and become unqualifiedly identified with the victims of racism in India. There can be no authentic Christian theology in India unless it focuses on the empowerment of the marginalized including the victims of racism.

God has taken the side of the marginalized including the victims of racism. Therefore, we must now critically re-evaluate the history of theology in India whether it has sided with the oppressor (even if it is by remaining silent).

Racism 'Within'

It is often said that "Racism is essentially born out of a lack of knowledge or more accurately, being misinformed." **I disagree!** Because there is a deliberate, informed and educated but very subtle racism that is prevalent in India today. This does not arise from 'Out there' but right 'Within.' It begins within our homes, schools, society, and church. Believe it or not racism is part of our upbringing. From childhood, we are brought up by demonizing the Other, isn't? Our jokes, popular sayings, caricatures, movies, are all replete with racist tendencies. We name the Other as *chinki, madrasi, mallu, lungi-wala, tsümar* etc., etc. Where do we learn all these? In specialized schools or institutions? No, right in our homes, and society. But unfortunately, the self-supremacy within a particular society continues to often go unspoken and unaddressed. It is time that we start holding ourselves accountable for the ways we keep the vicious cycle of racism going. We must begin to embrace an unchanging reality: human beings come in many shades, and the diversity simply adds to the vibrancy of our culture.

Conclusion: Where do we go from here?

We have noted that racism in all forms is evil and it has to be confronted and rejected. It becomes imperative on us as Christians to take the lead in the eradication of this sin. Biblical mandate, critical theological deliberations, church and its ethical life, law of the land, and basic common sense for human dignity forces us to confront and eliminate the evil of racism from our societies.

Is there a ready-made solution for the eradication of this menace? No, we do not have. Nevertheless, as Christians we are mandated to confront and reject this sin called racism from our society. How to go about it? I want to offer three simple suggestions: Talking, Confronting and Befriending.[42]

Talking

Let us start talking (and writing) about it. As Indians, we stand shamelessly exposed that we are one of the most racist nations in the world. Let us face it. There ought to be discussions on this issue both at the grass-root and at the academic levels. Pulpits should become radically active in preaching about it. Space should be provided both in the church and elsewhere where we should ask folks within society, church to share stories of racism within the context of our workplaces, institutions. Also, in this present wave of redefining our history and heroes from the past, why not we incorporate the histories and social systems of the North-East into our school textbooks and syllabus? The Battle of Kohima, which was the turning point of the eastern campaign during the Second World War, or the battles between the Mughals and the Ahom kingdom, so that we may learn a shared history, an inclusive history rather than have 'our' history versus 'their' history. For this the tourism sector of North-East India should be developed so that people from rest of India can experience the natural beauty and neglected history. Theological communities in India need to take up this matter seriously in it's theologizing in the classroom, chapel, outreach ministries, and writings.

Confronting

Political correctness should not push the issue of race under the carpet. Well, that has been the case till now in India. We need to face the reality and do what it takes. To recognise that racism exists

42 I have borrowed these three terms from Lamb, *God Behaving Badly: Is the God of the Old Testament Angry, Sexist, and Racist?*, 90-92.

in this country and that many unintended actions might emanate from racism can be a good place to start fighting the problem. To be oblivious (ignorant) of these issues or to deny its existence is to be complicit in the discriminatory regime. Also, the reason for fighting against racism is not because it is practised against 'our' own citizens but because it is wrong regardless of whether the victims of racism are citizens of the country or not. One way to be critical of racism is to recognise and make visible the presence of racism rather than merely resorting to legalistic means to curb this discrimination.

Jesus confronted it (cf. Luke 4, 10) through his ministry, message and life. So did the Early Church (Acts 15). A 'small' yet powerful way to confront it is by critically engaging with the racist tendencies at homes, churches, and institutions especially in our 'loose' talks (jokes, caricaturing, naming) about Others.

Befriending

Racism breeds in mono-cultural contexts. 'Difference' is considered an intruder therefore, not accepted and tolerated. A simple yet powerful way of challenging racism is: Making friends with people from other backgrounds. A 'multi-cultural living together' is a proposal that we can think of. In such a living all kinds of problems and difficulties are brought to the table (where openness for growth, communication and humanity is the ultimate criteria) for continuous dialogue and acting in solidarity. Biblical accounts are replete with stories of practicing radical hospitality towards people of different races like the 'Good Samaritan.' This befriending should be encouraged in our homes, societies, churches, and institutions.

I want to conclude the address by quoting from the Catholic Church of Belgium's declaration on racism: *Migrants and Refugees in our Midst* (1995). It reads: "the engagement of parishes and of Christian action groups on behalf of migrants and refugees is a touchstone for the authenticity of their Christianity."[43] Radical Openness to **strangers** is a criterion for authentic Christian life. This principle of openness for the Other can save religious communities and systems from absolutizing the acquired insights in such a way that they become no longer questionable from the outside by the

43 Pollefeyt, "Racism and Christian Belief: A Theological Reflection," 32.

Other. This radical openness leads to an endless search for truth and justice, by questioning the biased and temporary insights of the religious communities again and again. It is our contention here that such kind of religiousity should be encouraged and promoted not only because it works against racism, but even more it discloses the richness of the religious experience in always new contexts.

1

Some Thoughts on "Racism" from the Old Testament Pentateuch

Temsuyanger[1]

Introduction

In our contemporary world 'racism' remains a crucial challenge. Media coverage, government actions, and academic studies, have drawn attention to the persistent evils of racial, ethnic, and nationalistic prejudices in different parts of the world. Such persistent evil may even affect the church and withdraw the privilege of the church to be the salt of the earth. Racism is one of the ugliest features which give the growing interdependence of humankind its destructive and oppressive shape. The most obvious point to make about racism in general is one's prejudicial attitudes and behavior toward the ethnic or cultural "other," which is harmful, poisonous, and sinful. Caricatures and stereotyping of a racial or ethnic group is derived from ignorance, fear and 'xenophobia'[2] that reinforces negative attitudes, half-truths and lies, resulting in the exclusion of individuals

1 Mr. Temsuyanger teaches Old Testament at the Clark Theological College, Mokokchung, Nagaland.

2 "Xenophobia: a negative attitude and behavior against people and groups and outsiders of all types who are alien and different. Xenophobes hate the language, culture, clothing, and nationalities of others. Racism, on the other hand, hates the 'race' and 'descent,' whereby both naturally can go hand in hand. They mostly do, but it does not have to be the case." See Thomas Schirrmacher,

or groups from realizing their fullest potential in social, economic and political spheres. The consideration of this topic is divided into two main sections: the first section addresses the concepts of race and nation in the Bible and offers a theological reflection. The second focuses on the mega-narratives of Patriarchs, Exodus, and Joshua to invoke some ethical and theological questions and challenges pose by these mega-narratives. And finally, a contemporary challenge is highlighted to provoke some thoughts for the readers.

Race and Nation in the Bible

Modern ideas of racism were foreign to the biblical writers. For the biblical writers, 'race' in popular sense of today's world seems to be a non-concept. However, racism in the sense of some cultures, viewing themselves as superior, was certainly an issue in biblical times. For Greeks, foreigners unfamiliar with the Greek language and culture were regarded as barbarians; for Jews, non-Jews were regarded as Gentiles (i.e., pagans). In addition, the Bible indicates the diversity of people and nation that populate the earth. There are about 1,972 occurrences of ethnic designations in the Old Testament, conveyed by gentilic nouns such as Egyptians, Cushites, Philistines, Assyrians, etc.[3] Similarly, the New Testament also contains a variety of terms indicating ethnic, national, or racial affiliations. The list of pilgrims present in Jerusalem on Pentecost may be illustrative: Parthians, Medes, Elamites, etc. (Acts 2:9). Thus, it becomes apparent that the Bible has much to say about race and nations.

gôy (555 times) and *'am* (1866 times) are the common terms used in the Old Testament to convey the idea of race or ethnicity. In spite of considerable overlap, *gôy* designates nations and people as political and social entities, whereas *'am* stresses on kinship and more often refers to Israel as God's people. The word *lĕ' ôm* (31 times) often occurs in parallel with *gôy* in the prophetic literature

Racism, The WEA Global Issues Series, Volume 8 (Bonn: Verlag für Kultur und Wissenschaft Culture and Science Publisher, 2011), 17.

3 Elias Brasil de Souza, "Who is My Neighbor?": Some Thoughts on Racism and Nationals, https://adventistbiblicalresearch.org/sites/default/files/pdf/who%20is%20My%Neighbor_0.pdf (29/10/2015).

and Psalms.[4] Occurring in both Hebrew and Aramaic, the term,' *ummâ* (7 times) means "nation," "tribe," "people." The words *šēbeṭ* (190 times) and *matteh* (252 times) may designate "tribe," while *mišpāḥâ* (303 times) indicates the subdivision of a tribe and is mostly translated as "family."[5]

Diversity of Cultures in the Creation Text

Then God said, 'Let us make humankind in our image, according to our likeness . . . So God created humankind in his own image, in the image of God he created them; male and female he created them. God blessed them and said to them, 'Be fruitful and increase in number; fill the earth . . . (Gen 1: 26-28)

This is the written account of Adam's line. When God created humankind, he made them in the likeness of God. He created them male and female he created them, and blessed them. And when they were created, he called them 'humankind. (Gen 5: 1-2)

From one ancestor, he made all nations to inhabit the whole earth, and he allotted the times of their existence and the boundaries of the places where they would live. (Acts 17: 26)

The Hebrew Scripture shares the belief that all men and women are descended from one set of parents. 'Adam called his wife's name Eve, because she was the mother of all living.' St Paul's speech in Athens also substantiates, 'God made out of one every nation of human kind to dwell all over the earth' (Acts 17: 26). Secondly, the so-called table of nations (Gen 10) spells out the fact that all nations are in fact the descendants of these two human beings, the first man and the first woman. This provides an overview of human race and their ethnic groups at the early stages of world history. Thirdly, so far as humankind is concerned, there is only one group and it is with this group that the universal, Noachic covenant is made (Gen 9), on the basis of a single divine law about the sanctity of life, so that, whatever privileges the so-called the "chosen people" may later receive, the

4 Duane L. Christensen, "Nations," ed. David Noel Freedman, *The Anchor Bible Dictionary* (New York, NY: Doubleday, 1992), 4:1037.

5 C. J. H. Wright, "Family," ed. David Noel Freedman, *The Anchor Bible Dictionary* (New York, NY: Doubleday, 1992), 2:761-764.

fundamental fact is that God is in an eternal covenant relationship with all human beings on the fourfold basis of creation, moral law, judgment in history, and grace.

Fourthly, a close examination of genealogical lists indicates that a variety of nation and people forms the backdrop for subsequent promises that the nations of the earth would be blessed. The desirability of a diverse ethnic group and nation appears to be an implied mandate to "fill the earth" (Gen 9: 2). This may be explained when the builders of Babel met with God's judgment (Gen 11:1–9). When they resisted God's directive to fill the earth, God confused their language and scattered them all over the face of the earth. This brought about the diversity of families, nations, and ethnic groups, and eventually filled the earth by not only splitting the humanity into diverse families and peoples but also into vocations, abilities, and cultures.

Biblical notion of Creation clearly echoes that God is actively involved on behalf of nations and families of the earth as the plan of God's salvation unfolds. On the ground of Creation, there is no place for superiority of one group over another, because Creation clearly affirms the unity as well as the dignity of all humankind. On top of that the diversity of human cultures, races and nationalities bears the witness that all are created in the 'image of God.' Creation further makes it clear that the fall of humankind has not only affected God and humans' relationship, but it has also driven a wedge between humans and their fellow beings. And, as different groups of people become more and more alienated from God, they develop their own worldviews which result in racism, ethnocentrism, genocide, imperialism, etc., the consequences of which are oppression and destruction of the "other."

The biological scientific definition also clearly affirms the biblical notion of Creation. Recent genetic investigations from around the world have brought to light the astonishing genetic similarity of all people. At the DNA level all people are of one race, not of several. "The results of modern genetics have unobjectionably demonstrated that there are no different human races, and rather that there is only one species of mankind."[6] This affirmation is clear from the fact that all human groups share the same type of blood, are inter-fertile and can receive and donate organs across so-called racial boundaries.[7] All human groups are "one blood" as the Bible teaches.

The Patriarchal, Exodus, Conquest, and the Canaanites

I am the Lord, who brought you out of Ur of the Chaldeans to give you this land to take possession of it. (Gen 15: 7)

When my angel goes in front of you, and brings you to the Amorites, the Hittites, the Perizzites, the Canaanites, the Hivites, and the Jebusites, and ***I blot them out****, you shall not bow down to their gods, or worship them, or follow their practices, but* ***you shall utterly demolish them*** *and break their pillars in pieces.* (Exo 23: 23-24)

When the Lord your God brings you into the land that you are about to enter and occupy, and he clears away many nations before you, the Hittites, the Girgashites, the Amorites, the Canaanites, the Perizzites, the Hivites, and the Jebisites, seven nations mightier and more numerous than you, and when the Lord your God gives them over to you and ***you defeat them****, then* ***you must utterly destroy them. Make no covenant with them and show them no mercy.*** (Deut 7: 1-2)

But as for the towns of these peoples that the Lord your God is giving you as an inheritance, you must not let anything that breathes remain alive. You shall ***annihilate*** *them-the Hittites and the Amorites, the Canaanite and the Perizzites, the Hivites and the Jebusites-just as the Lord your God has commanded.* (Deut 20: 16-17)

Joshua took Makkedah on that day, and struck it and its king with the edge of the sword; he utterly destroyed every person in it; he left no one remaining. And he did to the king of Makkedah as he had done to the king of Jericho. (Josh 10: 28)

---

6 Nicht "Rassen" schaffen Rassismus, sondern Rassismus schafft "Rassen", http://www.ekr-cfr.ch/themen/00023/index.html?lang=de.

7 Cf. Thomas Schirrmacher, *Racism*, 19ff. Due to the use of the word "race" with a biological sense in racist ideologies, scholars have tended to abandon this word in favor of the term "ethnicity," in which culture, not biological, is the primary category to distinguish groups of people.

The Patriarchal, Exodus, and Conquest narratives describe the decisive history of the people of Israel. Both Jewish and Christian, and also to some extend the Muslim community, had appropriated these scriptures for their faith edification and instruction. The theological, ethical and historical issues surrounding these narratives have been the most fundamental concern in academia as well in the Church realm. One of the significant questions posed by the modern scholars and readers especially from the so-called the Third World is: Can the history of Palestine free itself from a past claimed and dominated by Israel? On this crucial issue K. W. Whitelam observes that the Israelite history, under the influence of biblical studies, has dominated the Palestinian setting to such an extent that it has virtually silenced all the other aspects of the history of the region. In his words,

> Biblical studies have formed part of the complex arrangement of scholarly, economic, and military power by which Palestinians have been denied a contemporary presence or history....Any recognition of the context in which biblical historian and archeologists work, the contemporary struggle for land and self-determination, is absent."[8]

He further observes that "The problem of Palestinian history has remained unspoken within biblical studies, silenced by the invention of ancient Israel in the image of the European nation state. Only after we have exposed the implications of this invention will Palestinian history be freed from the constraints of biblical studies and the discourse that has shaped it."[9] Unfortunately, even in the interpretative history it is least recognized that Palestine was occupied by diversity of peoples group. Thus, he concludes that "For too long Palestinian history has been a (minor) subset of biblical studies dominated by the biblically inspired histories and archaeologies of

---

8 K. W. Whitelam, *The Invention of Ancient Israel: The Silencing of Palestinian History* (London: Routledge, 1997), 226.

9 K. W. Whitelam, *The Invention of Ancient Israel*, 36.

ancient Israel"[10] and "Western scholarship has invented ancient Israel and silenced Palestinian history."[11]

One of the factors responsible for silencing the Palestinian history in the interpretative process is because of the presence of violent polemical statements and ideologies in regard to/for 'others' in the canonical Jewish Scripture. Unfortunately, the presence of such polemical statements has evoked serious ethical and theological questions, concurrently the issue of human rights in today's context. Palestinian historian like Nur Masalha questions the Hebrew biblical narratives that contain menacing ideologies and racist, xenophobic and militaristic tendencies.[12] The inspired texts appear not only justifying the occupation of others land, but also command bloodshed, ethnic cleansing and other crimes against humanity on the condition that the texts form a part of God's revealed plan.[13] Such polemical statements in the mega-narratives have further fueled into the continuation of conflicts for centuries. Therefore, many modern scholars are uncomfortable with some of the narratives that appear genocidal, which require a serious re-look from a new perspective with fresh, contemporary and authentic interpretation.

Many of the stories in the Patriarchal, Exodus, and Conquest tradition are the preserved of old memories, folk tales, myths, and aetiological anecdotes. The way they are compiled discloses that they serve the ideological and theological agendas of the late-Iron II authors.[14] Recent scholarships hold that these mega-narratives are the literary work of the late monarchic times or even later. In this position, Israel Finkelstein argues,

10 K. W. Whitelam, *The Invention of Ancient Israel,* 2.

11 K. W. Whitelam, *The Invention of Ancient Israel,* 3.

12 Nur Masalha, "Reading the Bible with the Eyes of the Canaanites: Neo-Zionism, Political Theology and the Land Traditions of the Bible (1967 to Gaza 2009)," *Holy Land Studies* 8/1 (May, 2009), 55-108.

13 Duncan Macpherson, "The Politics of Preaching the Promised Land for the Canaanites," *Political Theology*, 10/1 (2009), 76.

14 Israel Finkelstein, "Patriarchs, Exodus, Conquest: Fact or Fiction?" SBL *Archeology and Biblical Studies* 17, edited by Brian B. Schmidt (Atlanta: Society of Biblical Literature, 2007), 55.

> ...the "standardized" literary works narrating the history of Israel (in contrast to scattered, contradictory, and partial oral traditions) must have been written in an urban society, one with a high level of knowledge, sophistication, and literacy among the elite and the circle around it. They must have been written when the community was already quit advanced from the socio-political point of view and they must have been written in a period when literary spread not only in the capital, but also to the countryside of the kingdom....these conditions did not materialize in Judah and Jerusalem before the late-eight century B.C.E.[15]

From the perspective of the kingdoms of Israel and Judah we find a colorful presentation of human map of the ancient West Asia in the Patriarchal stories. Primarily the narratives are regarded as a literary attempt to redefine the unity of the people of Israel, rather than as an actual historical presentation of the lives of the Patriarchal characters living more than a millennium earlier. The choice of Canaan as the Promised Land for Abraham and his descendants, and Abraham as a great man to establish a prosperous nation and a blessing to the entire world are appealed to the people of exilic and post-exilic times. However, such a theological and ideological presentation poses difficult theological and ethical questions.[16]

The historicity of Exodus and Joshua are highly debatable, since the departure of the people of Israel from Egypt and the occupation of the land of Canaan are hardly verifiable in extrabiblical sources. Hebrew Bible research holds "that there is complete absence of any external written documents testifying to Israel's presence and subjugation in Egypt, to her migration from that

---

15 Israel Finkelstein, "Digging for the Truth: Archeology and the Bible" in *The Quest for the Historical Israel: Debating Archaeology and the History of Early Israel*, by Israel Finkelstein and Amihai Mazar, edited by Brian B. Schmidt (Leiden. Boston, 2007), 17. He emphasizes that in the study of ancient Israel one should rather view the texts "from the center," which means, the text should not be read as a sequential history chronologically, but in reverse-from the time of the writing back to the more remote periods of history.

16 See for further discussion, Laiu Facchhai, *The Land must be Distributed Equally: The Promised and Covenant aspects of Land in the Old Testament* (Delhi: ISPCK, 2009), 17ff.

land, or to her conquest and her settlement there."[17] Exodus story is based on some remote memories in the reality of the thirteenth century BCE, rather on a good knowledge of the geographical and environmental conditions of the territories.[18] There is also a heavy hand of Deuteronomistic Historian, who must have taken the old folktales and fragmented memories and incorporated them in the compilation.[19] The book of Joshua is believed to be tended towards a polemical purpose, against Assyrian totalitarian and brutal militarization.[20] In order to oppose Assyrian hegemony the Deuteronomistic Historian agreed to militarize and brutalize their own religious traditions, defending the notion of Yahweh's supremacy over the gods of the Assyrian and legitimizing Israel's occupation of the land of Canaan. Thus, the Conquest narrative is almost complete expression of the political and theological ideology of the late monarchic authors.

Now, it is quite reasonable to concur from the above discussion that the mega-narratives are literary-rhetorical product of late monarchic time (or even later), and the texts must have served the theological and ideological needs and agendas of the authors. Hence, the narratives are not necessarily about their historical factuality, but about their literary-rhetorical function and agenda of the authors. Many of the stories in the texts are constructed in such a way befitting the ideology of the authors. Therefore, R. Warrior has rightly commented, "Confronting the conquest stories as a narrative rather

---

17 Nahum M. Sarna, "Exodus, Book of," in *The Anchor Bible Dictionary*, Vol. 2, ed. David Noel Freedman (New York: Doubleday, 1992), 96-97.

18 Amihai Mazar, "The Patriarchs, Exodus, and Conquest Narratives in Light of Archeology," SBL *Archeology and Biblical Studies* 17, 61.

19 Israel Finkelstein, "Patriarchs, Exodus, Conquest: Fact or Fiction?" 53.

20 It appears that such a trouble texts have negative theological values, but looking from the social perspective of the authors, they have positive social values. It teaches us more about the authors than about God. Unfortunately the book like Joshua was used to justify, among others, the institution of slavery in the West in the past centuries. Cf. P. Joseph Titus, "Images of God: With Particular reference to Violence in the Bible," Nation Conference on "Hermeneutics from a Palestinian's Perspective," BTESSC, Bangalore (2014), 6ff. (Unpublished paper)

than a historical problem is especially important."[21] So the questions posed by such mega-narratives are: Is such literary-rhetorical devices allow ethnic cleansing and imperialism? How these texts constructed difference: Are there dialogue and mutual interdependence, or condemnation and replacement of all that is foreign? What does the narratives meant to the implied readers?

Challenges of Mega-Narratives

The following observations can infer from the mega-narratives: first, the narratives authorizes traveling from one land to another; second, the natives construct the image of the targeted land and its people as immoral, unethical, barbarians, cursed and underdeveloped; third, the narratives construct the identity of the people who colonize the targeted land; fourth, the narratives treat the resident as aliens in their own land; and fifth, the narratives sanction the expansionist ambition. In the context of such literary construct, Musa M. Dube, in her reading of Exodus-Joshua stories from the post colonial feminist perspective openly declares,

> Clearly, the open admission that the Promised Land is inhabited underlines God as authorizer....the characterization of God as the initiator and hero in the narrative is a rhetorical device that sanctifies the acts of imperialism. The Exodus anti-conquest ideology maintains its innocence by appealing to the highest, unquestionable authority of God. If God gives the land, then, regardless of whether it is inhabited, the whole act is just.[22]

Such narratives invite the implied readers to nod approvingly to God's act of genocide and imperialism. Certainly, it is a portrayal of God who is in conflict with self, which is revealed in the exodus and by Jesus-the God of liberation and social justice. Critiquing the presence of such menacing theological notion in the Bible Robert Eisen argues that, "Whatever sophisticated explanations one may give to soften the violence of the Bible, it remains a text that has

---

21 http://archiver.rootsweb.ancestry.com/th/read/AMERIND-US-SE/2001-05/0990268845

22 Musa W. Dube, *Postcolonial Feminist Interpretation of the Bible* (St. Louis, Missouri: Chalic Press, 2000), 65.

encourage bloodshed....Bible seems to giving the Israelites license to take violent actions against their enemies even when not explicitly commanded to do so."[23] Exodus-Joshua narratives give us a clear portrait and notion that the victimized losers in the history somehow have the right to be winners by victimizing other, in turn, even to the extent of exterminating the inhabitants by force.[24] In other words, the liberated Israelis used the same mechanisms of oppression vis-à-vis their neighbour.

"Ethnic cleansing is a well-defined policy of a particular group or person to systematically eliminate another group from a given territory on the basis of religious, ethnic or national origin. Such a policy involves violence and is very often connected with military operations. It is to be achieved by all possible means, from discrimination to extermination...."[25] In light of the definition and the above discussion it is reasonably certain that the narratives are imperializing and genocidal, because they expressly focused on taking and maintaining power over the foreigners and their inhabited lands.

In Pentateuch the land of Canaan is identified with acts of sexual aberrations. The land is identified with homosexuality (Gen 9: 20-26; 19: 5-8) and bestiality. In Leviticus alone Israel is warned at least seven times not to behave as the nation that is inhabited by Canaanites (Lev 18: 3, 24, 26, 27, 29, 30). Throughout the book of Deuteronomy one finds a strong polemic against religious practice of Canaanites (Deut 13: 15; 12: 13; 18: 10; 14: 3-21). But it seems there is no extra biblical evidence to show that the Canaanites were worse in sexual immorality. By over emphasizing the sex crimes and fertility cult practices, the redactors of the Hebrew Bible attempt

---

23 Quoted in J. H. Muthuraj, "A Voice is Heard in Ramah Weeping and Great Mourning: An Indian Looks at the Palestinian Question," Nation Conference on "Hermeneutics from a Palestinian's Perspective" BTESSC, Bangalore (2014), 12. (Unpublished paper)

24 Cf. Musa W. Dube, *Postcolonial Feminist Interpretation of the Bible,* 56ff.

25 Ilan Pappe, *The Ethnic Cleansing of Palestine* (London: One World Publications, 2006), 1.

to stigmatize the Canaanites.[26] "The antagonism between Canaan and Israel covered all aspects of human life from family to social and political organization, from structures of ownership to faith and rituals."[27] In this stream of understanding the Israel attitude towards the other nations and cultures was apparently intolerance, arrogance, exclusivistic, highly judgmental and self-centered.[28]

Palestinian liberation theologian like Robert Allen Warrior therefore, calls for the Christian reflection that places the Canaanites at the centre of theological thought, and to consider the violence and injustice rarely discovered in the critical works concerning the book of Exodus and others.[29] Another Palestinian theologian Stifan Ateek also comments that there are nationalistic tradition in the Bible largely in Joshua, Judges, 1 & 2 Samuel and 1 & 2 Kings. He argues, "....purely nationalistic and militaristic approach (in these books) aimed at regaining Jewish independence."[30] In the books the idea of 'violent God' falls in line with the nationalistic agenda of Israel through 'selection' theory and 'promise' of land.[31] Such supremacist ideology is perhaps having a powerful damage on the security of the people in Palestine even in today's context, which is a thread to world peace. Identifying the militant land traditions of the Bible which justify the destruction of the previous inhabitants, Alex Awad put forth fourfold challenge in today's context: "Are God's promises to ancient Israel unconditional? Are God's promise to ancient Israel perpetual, i.e., never ending? Do Old Testament prophecies relating to 'the land' under the old covenant continue to have significance and fulfillment within the framework of the new covenant? Does

---

26 J. Milcrom, *Leviticus 17-22, The Anchor Yale Bible* (New Haven: Yale University Press, 2008), 1520.

27 L. Legrand, *Bible on Culture* (Bangalore: TPI, 2001), 15.

28 Rui de Menezes, "Communalism in Ancient Israel," *Vidyajyothi* 56 (1992), 140.

29 M. A. De La Torre, *Liberation Theology for Armchair Theologians* (Kentucky: Westminster John Knox Press, 2013), 135.

30 Naim Stifan Ateek, *Justice and Only Justice: A Palestinian Theology of Liberation* (Maryknoll: Orbis Books, 1989), 94.

31 Naim Stifan Ateek, *Justice and Only Justice*, 94.

God have a special plan for the Jewish people different from that for other peoples?"[32]

Some of the Christian evangelical writers observe and feel that the genocidal and imperialism is inevitable in such texts. Some of the rationales for their arguments are: Canaanite genocide was necessary in order to prevent Israel from practicing idolatry (Deut 7: 2), because the God of Israel threatened with destruction if she practice idolatry (Deut 7: 4); God authorized conquest because of their detestable practices, so that the land may be claimed for the exclusive worship of Yahweh;[33] in the absence of Canaanite destruction God's messianic purpose through the Israel nation would not have accomplished; conquest was a divine reenactment of creation; conquest as a instructive device; and conflict to be understood not merely on the physical realm but also on the cosmic and spiritual realms.

Contemporary Challenge

Religious Zionism is considered as one of the ideological instruments for religious fundamentalism in the context of Israel-Palestine conflict. Torah centric approach to scripture is said to be instrumental for the emergence of Rabbinic Judaism which produced the Talmud[34] and Mishnah. Biblical Israel as mentioned in Torah is equated with the

32 "A Palestinian Theology of the Land," in *The Land Cries Out: Theology of the Land in the Israeli-Palestinian Context*, S. J. Munayer and L. Loden eds. (Wipf and Stock Publisher, 2011), 202.

33 Some early Protestant missions in North America regarded the dispossession of the lands of the native "Indian" as a divine task necessary for turning the land into the "promised land."

34 Some violent texts in Talmud can be cited: "When the Messiah comes every Jew will have 2800 slaves" (*Simeon Haddarsen, fol.* 56-D); That the Jewish nation is the only nation selected by God, while all remaining ones are contemptible and hateful. That all property of other nations belongs to the Jewish nation, which consequently is entitled to seize upon any scruples (*Schulchan Aruch, Choszen Hamiszpat,* 348); "If a goy killed a goy or a Jew he is responsible, but if a Jew killed a goy he is not responsible" (*Tosefta, Aboda Zara,* VIII, 5); "Kill the Goyim by any means possible" (*Choshen Ha'mispat* 425: 50); "Do not save Goyim in danger of death. Show no mercy to the Goyim" (*Hilkkoth Akum* X1). *Quotes from the Bible, Talmud and Zohar (Kabbala),* author unknown. https://archievc.org/details/QuotesFromTtheBibleTalmudAndZoharkabbala (18/08/2014).

contemporary Israel as a nation-state, which is a root for perpetuating and justifying Israel annexation of Palestinian land. By interpreting contemporary Israel as biblical God's promise land people already living in that land were not at all counted, but understood as *a land without people*. Reading and interpretation of the past in relation to the present has encouraged religious fundamentalism.[35]

In the background of Jews suffering in ghettos, holocaust killing, the guilt consciousness of European Christians conceived the idea of creating a new home land (a political idea) for Jewish people in Palestine. During colonialism and imperialism some evangelical circles had taken up the idea of linking the biblical Israel with the contemporary Israel to bring them to the land of Palestine. Such an act was viewed by the evangelicals as the fulfillment of biblical prophecy.[36] Though, such move had started in the 19th century of modern era, even to this day the ordinary Christians knowingly and unknowing consider the contemporary Israel for spiritual Israel of the biblical times. The theme of God's chosen people is used to support today's Israelis nationalistic tradition. The nationalistic spirit is induced whoever visits the land of Palestine especially the Christians. The tourists are taken to the different memorial sights inducing their minds to see modern Israel as the only and the worst sufferer of modern times.

Explaining the ideology of Zionism of the 19th century as a reason for crisis in Palestine, Ilan Pappe says, "Zionism was not... the only case in history in which a colonialist project was pursued in the name of national or otherwise non-colonist ideals. Zionists relocated to Palestine at the end of a century in which Europeans controlled mush of Africa, the Caribbean, and other places in the name of 'progress' or idealism..."[37] Some Jews in Europe stressed

---

35 Cf. Praveen PS, Perumalla, "Justice and Peace in the Context of Conflicts of Plurality of Faith: Persuasions in the Scripture," Nation Conference on "Hermeneutics from a Palestinian's Perspective" BTESSC, Bangalore (2014), 6. (Unpublished paper)

36 Cf. Praveen PS, Perumalla, "Justice and Peace in the Context of Conflicts of Plurality of Faith," 6ff.

37 Quoted in Amjad Alquasis, "The Ongoing Nakba: Continues forcible displacement of the Palestinian people," in an unpublished paper (July, 2012),

upon the universalistic character of Judaism drawing upon the universalistic understanding of God, by doing so the Torah centric approach did comply with the 'hostile European Christianity' of the 19th century.[38]

Zionism has assumed different political meaning with the onset of Christian pro-Zionism at the modern times. Christian pro-Zionist dispensationalists hold that humankind has entered the final period, the Last Days, or End Times. They interpret current events and the world situation in the light of biblical prophecy. They believe that the End Times are marked by the birth of the modern state of Israel, thus support physical and political restoration of the entire Holy land, geographic Palestine, to the Jewish people as an exclusive possession. This ideology has become an influential force in US politics.[39] Zionism relies on Biblical Studies, a field that allows for loose religious dogmatic interpretations, especially when evidences are seriously lacking. One way the Biblical Studies approach can establish the myth of ancient Israel is by arbitrarily using the Jewish biblical tradition as the main source of interpretation. Thus, contemporary Christians must resist and confront the violence that is injected in the canonized texts as well as in the interpretative process. It is necessary to dismantle the Zionist ideology and Western interest by constructing myths for political purpose that leave the Palestinians out of moral concern. This has to be done by re-evaluating from the perspective of the victims.

Conclusion

This paper concludes with the words of Mahatma Gandhi on the issues of Jew-Arab relations, the voice of Christians in Palestine, and the report of the World Council of Churches:

> And now a word to the Jews in Palestine. I have no doubt that they are going about it in the wrong way. The Palestine of the

BADIL from Ilan Pappe, "Zionism as Colonialism: A Comparative View of Diluted Colonialism in Asia AND Africa," in *South Atlantic Quarterly* 107: 4, (2008), 612.

38 Naim Stifan Ateek, *Justice and Only Justice,* 95.

39 Cf. J. H. Muthuraj, "A Voice is Heard in Ramah Weeping and Great Mourning," 9ff.

> Biblical conception is not a geographical tract. It is in their hearts. But if they must look to the Palestine of geography as their national home, it is wrong to enter it under the shadow of the British gun. A religious act cannot be performed with the aid of the bayonet or the bomb. They can settle in Palestine only by the goodwill of the Arabs....The same God who rules the Arab heart who rules the Jewish heart....They will find the world opinion in their favor in their religious aspiration....I am not defending the Arab excesses. I wish they had chosen the way of non-violence in resisting what they rightly regarded as an unwarrantable encroachment upon their country. But according to the accepted canons of right and wrong, nothing can be said against the Arab resistance in the face of overwhelming odds. (M. Gandhi)[40]

> Our word to the Churches of the world is firstly a word of gratitude for the solidarity you have shown toward us in word, deed and presence among us. It is a word of praise for many Churches and Christians who support the right of the Palestinian people for self determination....However, it is also a call to repentance; to revisit fundamentalist theological positions that support certain unjust political options with regard to the Palestinian people. It is a call to stand alongside the oppressed and preserve the word of God as good news for all rather than to turn into a weapon with which to slay the oppressed....We ask our sister Churches not to offer a theological cover-up for the injustice we suffer, for the sin of the occupation imposed upon us. Our question to our brothers and sisters in the Churches today is: Are you able to help us get us free back, for this is the only way you can help the two peoples attain justice, peace, security and love? (Palestinian Christians)[41]

The World Council of Churches (WCC) general secretary Olav F. Tveit also expressed deep concern over the renewed wave of violence in Jerusalem in recent days. He stressed, "The WCC stands firmly with Christians in the Holy Land in our conviction that the

40 L. A. Gorden, "Indian Nationalist Ideas about Palestine and Israel" *Jewish Social Studies*, Vol. 37, no. ¾ (Summer-Autumn, 1975), 225.

41 *Kairos Palestine: A Moment of Truth*, Study Series No. 2 (Bangalore: BTESSC, 2014), 21-22.

illegal occupation of the Palestinian Territories must be brought to an end – not as a pre-condition for an end to violence, but as an essential foundation for any long-term, sustainable and just peace in the region." With the vision of a "pilgrimage of justice and peace" as promoted by the WCC 10th Assembly in 2013 at Busan, the primary focus of the "pilgrimage of justice and peace" for 2016 will be the Middle East, with an emphasis on Israel and Palestine."[42]

---

42 Ranjan Solomon, Palestine Israel Ecumenical Forum, https://in-mg61.mail.yahoo.com/neo/launch?.rand=fo66l6e9cs7pi#4340635282 (29/10/2015).

2

Jews, Greeks and Barbarians in Romans 1:14 and 16
Paul's Response to Ethnocentrism

B. J. Syiemlieh[1]

Introduction

In 1977, E. P. Sander initiated a movement in Pauline studies which was later labelled as "the new perspective on Paul."[2] He was joined in 1982 by James D. G. Dunn who coined this term[3] and the movement was later popularized by prominent New Testament scholars like N. T. Wright.[4] This movement marked a paradigm shift in Pauline studies in that the interpretation of Paul's letters was ejected out of the old perspective governed by the Lutheran-Reformed theological framework. In brief, the basic premise of this movement is that Paul was not against the legalism of the Jewish law but that he was only questioning the ethnocentrism inherent in the observances of

1 Dr. Brightstar Jones Syiemlieh is the Principal of the John Roberts Theological Seminary, Shillong and an Associate Professor in the Department of New Testament.

2 *Paul and Palestinian Judaism: A Comparison of Patterns of Religions* (Philadelphia: Fortress Press, 1977).

3 "The New Perspective on Paul," *Bulletin of the John Ryland Library*, vol. 65 (1983): 95-122; *Jesus, Paul and the Law: Studies in Mark and Galatians* (London: SPCK, 1990); *The New Perspective on Paul: Collected Essays* WUNT 85 (Tubingen: Mohr/Siebeck, 2005).

4 *Paul: In Fresh Perspective* (Minneapolis: Fortress Press, 2009).

some aspects of the Jewish law like the observance of circumcision and the observance of dietary laws. Since, the old perspective had indirectly projected Paul as being anti-Semitic, one of the side effects of the new perspective movement is that it paves the way towards redefining Paul's attitude towards the Jews. Taking a cue from this paradigm shift, this paper will attempt to analyze Paul's references to the Jews, the Greeks and the barbarians in Romans 1:14 and 16. The hypothesis of this paper is that these references are socio-cultural markers which can unveil Paul's response to ethnocentric behaviour and attitudes inherent in society. Since, ethnocentrism is a key term used in this paper to describe social behaviour and social attitudes which are reflected in the socio-cultural markers, this paper will begin with a definition of the term ethnocentrism. This will be followed by a description of ethnocentrism in the first century Mediterranean world. Finally, an analysis of Rom 1:14 and 16 will be given to formulate Paul's response to ethnocentric behaviour and attitudes.

Defining Ethnocentrism

Though, popular writings in social sciences credit the American sociologist William Graham Sumner as the first to use the term ethnocentrism,[5] recent findings have shown that the term was first used by L. Glumpowicz, a Polish sociologist towards the end of the 19th century.[6] In his works, Glumpowicz described ethnocentrism as a "delusion" to geocentrism (the belief that the earth has the central position in the universe) and anthropocentrism (the belief that humans have the central position on the earth), but focusing on one's own ethnic group (nation, people). This belief in centrality is reflected in the view that the group is extraordinary, superior, and better in relation to any other group – and not only any other existing group, but any group that has ever existed.[7] Glumpowicz also exemplified his arguments by pointing to the writings of history in

5 *Folkways: A Study of the Sociological Importance of Usages, Manners, Customs, Mores, and Morals* (Boston, MA: Ginn and Company, 1906).

6 For details see Boris Bizumic, "Who Coined the Concept Ethnocentrism: A Brief Report," *Journal of Social and Political Psychology*, vol. 2 (2014): 3–10.

7 *Ibid.*, 3.

his time which were dominated by limited ethnocentric viewpoints. He says that "the largest part of historical writing so far actually has only sprung from this subjective need of human beings to glorify their own and nearest and at the same time humiliate and sully what is foreign and distant."[8]

William Graham Sumner adopted, popularized and developed the term to make it an important concept in social sciences. As of now, ethnocentrism is used to refer to behaviour and attitudes which consider one's own culture, language, belief and life style as central while that of others is accorded a less prominent role or is placed at or outside the margins. Ethnocentrism is closely related to other attitudinal indicators for racism, xenophobia, prejudice, mental closure, and, more generally, an authoritarian personality structure. It is widely used in research on social and political attitudes because it proves to be a very powerful and easily identifiable attitude that can be measured in a valid manner with a limited number of variables. Although, ethnocentric prejudice can be directed toward one specific outsider group, empirical research reveals that usually ethnocentrism is generalized toward all outsider groups.[9]

Though, ethnocentrism in popular parlance carries negative connotations, Melville J. Herkovits, a pioneer in cultural anthropology, opines that a moderate dose of ethnocentrism is healthy. His basic argument is that ethnocentrism is a point of view that one's way of life is to be preferred to that of others. Flowing logically from the process of early enculturation, he says that it characterizes the way individual feel about their own culture, whether or not they verbalize their feelings.[10] Though, this implies that every human is in one way or the other ethnocentric, yet caution must be taken against

---

8 Cited by Boris Bizumic, "Who Coined the Concept Ethnocentrism: A Brief Report," *Journal of Social and Political Psychology*, vol 2 (2014), 4 from L Gumplowicz, *Der Russenkampf: Sociologische Untersuchungen* [The racial struggle: Sociological studies] (Innsbruck, Austria: Wagner'sche Universitäts-Buchhandlung, 1883), 252-253.

9 Cf. March Hooghe, "Ethnocentrism," in *International Encyclopaedia of Social Sciences*, vol. 1 (Philadelphia: Macmillan, 2008), *passim.*

10 *Cultural Anthropology* (Knopf: New York, 1965), 356.

the dangers of being overtly ethnocentric in the sense of viewing and judging others through one's own cultural lenses.[11]

Ethnocentrism in the Social World of Pauline Christianity

Pauline Christianity was part of the first century Mediterranean world. As it is well known, this world was politically united by the Roman Empire but it was marked by diversity in terms of ethnicity, language, religion and culture. For instance, the provinces within the Roman Empire comprised of various ethnicities like the Romans, Athenians, Macedonians, Cretans, Scythians, Jews, Gauls, Medes and so on. Though, vernacular languages of the ethnic groups were in use, Greek was the *lingua franca* of the empire while Latin was the language of the Romans. Greek art and philosophy impressed upon the citizens of the empire. Greek religion, Roman religion, the mystery religions and Judaism were practiced by various groups. This feature of the Roman Empire can be gleaned from numerous references in the New Testament and Greek historians of the period apart from archaeological evidences.[12]

But as it is evident in most situations, it should be noted that diversity in the social world of Pauline Christianity also gave rise to the problem of ethnocentrism. For instance, Romans and Greeks from Athens considered themselves to be superior and looked down at others as foreigners and barbarians. Even among Greek, Athenians looked down at Macedonians as uncultured in Greek language and art.[13] Romans also differentiate a citizen from a foreigner or a slave just as it is common for Jews to identify others as gentiles. Here, it should be mentioned that the ethnocentric behaviour and attitude is not based only on ethnicity but works in combination with other social factors like language, religion and culture which

---

11 R. M. Keesing, *Cultural Anthropology: A Contemporary Perspective* (New York: Holt, Rinehart and Winston, 1981), 69.

12 Any standard book on introduction to the New Testament will provide information on this diversity within the Roman Empire of the first century. See Raymond E Brown, *An Introduction to the New Testament* (Bangalore: TPI, 2000), 55-93.

13 Michael Bakaoukas, "Tribalism and Racism among Ancient Greek: A Weberian Perspective," *Anistoriton Journal*, vol. 9 (2005): 1-15.

overlapped or are socially embedded with one another. Bruce Malina and Jerome H. Neyrey explain the problem of ethnocentrism in the social world of early Christianity by employing models from cultural anthropology. To cite an example, honor and shame is a model from cultural anthropology which is used to explain the intrinsic and innate behaviour and attitude of people in society. According to this model, every individual and group craves for honor and avoids being shamed upon. Honour is recognition, status and identity based on a number of factors like social standing, heredity, wealth, ethnicity, language, culture, religion, gender and so on. Since honour is valuable for a person or a group, and since every interaction between persons or groups is looked upon as a social contest, it is closely guarded and most often aggressively safeguarded so as to result in ethnocentric behaviour and attitude.[14] Therefore, the diversity in terms of ethnicity, language, religion and culture make ethnocentrism the hallmark of social behaviour and attitude in the social world of Pauline Christianity.

Jews, Greeks and Barbarians in Rom 1:14, 16: An Analysis

In Pauls letters, with the exception of Coll 3:11, the terms Jews (*Ioudaioi*), Greeks (*Hellenēs*) and barbarians (*babaroi*) appear concurrently only in these two passages in Rom 1:14 and 16. To be precise, Greeks and barbarians occur concurrently in v. 14 where as Jews and Greeks occur concurrently in v. 16. In the social context of Pauline Christianity where ethnocentrism is the hallmark of social behaviour and attitude, it is significant to note that the three terms when put together can create a highly charged atmosphere because they represent social groups which stand in opposition to one another. However, it must be noted that so far no attempt has been made to investigate the significance of this occurrence in the wider framework of the letter to the Romans or to Pauline theology except for the use of the first two terms to identify the audience of the letter.[15]

---

14 For details see Bruce Malina and Jerome H. Neyrey, *The New Testament World: Insights from Cultural Anthropology* (Atlanta: John Knox, 1981).

15 James D. G. Dunn, *Romans 1-8*, WBC 38A (Dallas, Texas: Word Books, 1988), xlv.

In the literary context of Rom 1, these references occur in a context where Paul makes mission statements. In v. 14, Paul states that he is indebted to both the Greeks and the barbarians for his success in reaching out to gentiles where as in v. 16 he makes a missional statement that the gospel should be proclaimed to both the Jews and the Greeks. In a highly charged and ethnocentric atmosphere of first century Mediterranean world where any sort of interaction between different social groups and ethnicities is frowned upon, an important question arises as to what are the implications of these statements? To answer this question, an explanation of the social exigencies of the three terms Jews (*Ioudaioi*), Greeks (*Hellenēs*) and barbarians (*babaroi*) as used in these passages is needed.

To begin with, the term Jew (*Ioudaios*) describes the social identity of an ethnic group with a distinct language, culture and religion.[16] In the context of the early Church, particularly the Pauline churches, it refers to an ethnic Jew who adheres to the demands of the Mosaic law and thus considers oneself as belonging to the group of God's chosen people (cf. Gal 2:13) in contrast to others who are identified as Greeks or gentiles standing outside the group of God's chosen people. At a glimpse, the statement in v. 16 which says that the gospel is the power of God for salvation to everyone who has faith, "to the Jew first and also to the Greek" appears to echo the ethnocentric view point of the Jews by giving primacy to the Jews to be the first recipients of the proclamation of the gospel. However, it should be noted that the same phrase ("to the Jew first and also to the Greek") is used when referring to divine judgement (2:9). Therefore, the use of the phrase ("to the Jew first and also to the Greek") with reference to both salvation and judgement neutralizes the ethnocentrism inherent therein. To substantiate his arguments, Paul would go on to redefine the identity of a true Jew not as a blind adherent of the demands of the Mosaic law but as one who adheres to the spirit behind it (2:21-29). Paul's balancing act to abrogate

16 Shaye J. D. Cohen, "Religion, Ethnicity and 'Hellenism' in the Emergence of Jewish Identity in Maccabean Palestine." In *Religion and Religious Practice in the Seleucid Kingdom*, edited by Pers Bilde, Troels Engberg-Pedersen, Lise Hannestad, and Jan Zahle (Aarhus University: Aarhus University Press, 1990), 205.

ethnocentrism can also be seen in his self-identification as a Jew (Phil 3:4-6) and his self-understanding to be an apostle to the gentiles (Rom 11:13).[17] Therefore, the use of the term Jew in Paul refers to the social identity of an ethnic group with a distinct language, culture and religion and it is in no way used to indicate superiority of the group over others.

The other term Greek (*Hellenēs*) describes the social identity of a person whose ethnicity, language and culture is linked to Greek. In the social world of early Christianity, it can also include a Hellenized inhabitant, that is, a person from another ethnic group who has embraced Greek language, culture and philosophy.[18] Since Greek language, ethnicity, culture and philosophy are social factors which were virtually absolutized so as to become predominant, it was common for Greeks in the first century to consider non-Greeks as barbarians.[19] Thus, the Greek self-understanding of being Greek, which is socially expressed in their dealing and interaction with non-Greek, is highly ethnocentric.

However, the Jews' perception of the term Greek is worth noting. Since for Jews, the Greek sphere is not confined only to language and culture but also included religion, the understanding of the term Greek by Jews approximates to gentile. Thus, when the high priest Jason adopted Greek language and culture and abandoned Jewish customs, he was called a Greek because to the Jews, religion and culture are inseparable.[20] As such, the Jews' perception of Greek also reflects ethnocentrism.

Though, there are instances where the term is used in a cultural sense to identify ethnic Greek and residents of Hellenistic towns and cities (AA 11:10; 14:1; 17:4), Paul always uses this term in opposition

---

17 Cf. Ben Witherington III, *The Paul Quest: The Renewed Search for the Jew of Tarsus* (Downers Grove, Illinois: InterVarsity Press, 1998), 57.

18 H. Windisch, "*Hellen*," *TDNT*, Abridged in One Volume by Geoffrey W. Bromiley, edited by Gerhard Kittel *et al.* (Grand Rapids, Michigan: William B. Eerdmans Publishing Company, 1985), 227.

19 H. Preisler, "*Hellen*," *TDNT*, vol. 11, edited by Gerhard Kittel, *et al.* (Grand Rapids, Michigan: William B. Eerdmans Publishing Company, 1974), 504-516.

20 Windisch, "*Hellen*," 227-228.

to the Jews so as to imply that Greeks are gentiles or Greeks are just like people of other nations who are not Jews (1 Cor 1:24; Gal 3:27-28).[21] However, it should be noted that there is nothing derogatory in the usage as the term Greek in Paul is used as an equal opposition of Jew. Indeed, in v. 14, Paul says that he is obliged or indebted to both Greeks and barbarians for his mission work where as in v. 16 he expresses his desire to proclaim the gospel to the Jews as well as to the Greeks. Therefore, Greeks in Paul are placed at par with Jews so as to deflate ethnocentric behaviour and attitudes.

Finally, the term barbarian (*barbaros*) is a derogatory label created by the Greek to identify non-Greek. To Greek, non-Greek are those whose ethnicity and ancestry is not linked to Greece; those who speak Greek badly and those who speak an unintelligible language to the Greek; those who are not familiar with Greek philosophy and culture. Besides, it also carries the meaning of being wild, crude, fierce and uncivilized.[22] To the Romans, a barbarian is one who is not a citizen of Rome or who resides outside the empire[23] where as for the Greeks, it refers to a person who does not speak Greek and who does not follow Greek culture.[24] According to Aristotle, barbarians within the Roman Empire were mostly slaves or slavish by nature (*Politics* 1:2-7; 3:14). As such, unlike Jews and Greeks, barbarians in the social world of the early Christianity refer to a group who are victims of ethnocentric groups.

In the writings of Paul, the term barbarian appears only in Rom 1:14 and Coll 3:11. In both instances, it can be noted that the negative overtone of the term is toned down. First, it is significant to note that barbarians in v. 14 are placed on an equal footing with the

21 C. E. B. Cranfield, *A Critical and Exegetical Commentary on the Epistle to the Romans*, ICC, vol. 2, (Edinburgh: T and T Clark, 1975), 90-91.

22 H. Windisch, "*Barbaros*," *TDNT*, vol. 1, edited by Gerhard Kittel, *et al.* (Grand Rapids, Michigan: William B. Eerdmans Publishing Company, 1976), 546-553.

23 Dean Flemming, Contextualization in the New Testament: Patterns for Theology and Mission (Downers Grove, Illinois: InterVarsity Press, 2005) 128–29.

24 James D. G. Dunn, *Romans 1-8*, WBC, vol. 38A (Dallas, Texas: Word Books, 1988), 33.

Greeks just as the consequent refrain of wise-foolish re-emphasizes. Second, though the clubbing of Greeks with barbarians is taken as an indication of the universal mission of Paul, the language of indebtedness can also be taken to imply that Paul is planning to extend his mission beyond Rome in partnership with these groups.[25] As if to give more impetus to what is stated in v. 14, Coll 3:11 totally abrogates any distinction between Greeks and barbarians. Hence, by abrogating and placing barbarians on par with Greeks, the ethnocentrism of the Greeks is subverted.

Ethnocentrism vis-a-vis the Contemporary Northeast Context

Since, the discussions are being made with reference to the frequent attacks against people of Northeast India in some metropolitan cities of India, it would be appropriate to discern the relevance of Paul's response to ethnocentrism vis-a-vis the Northeast context. However, while launching this quest, it is imperative to give a brief but analytical description of ethnocentrism in the context of Northeast India.

Like many societies with the distinctive traits of ancient societies, ethnocentrism in the contemporary context of Northeast India can be best analyzed at two levels of interaction, namely, the interaction between people of mainland India and the people of Northeast India in Northeast India and the interaction between the different groups of people in Northeast India. The main reason for attaching importance to these two levels is because this is where frequent social interaction takes place. Though, social sciences opine that every social interaction is a social contest, it should be noted that this is true for frequent social interaction between groups with different traits normally which results in friction and conflict whereas occasional interaction can be bonding and lead to socialization. Social interaction between like groups on the other hand is looked upon as normal and considered to be the norm.

In the wider Indian context, ethnocentrism is a thriving force because of the ethnic, linguistic, religious and cultural diversity of India. But with reference to the social interaction between people of Northeast India with people of mainland India in Northeast India,

25 James R. Harrison, "Paul's 'Indebtedness' to the Barbarian (Romans 1:14) in Latin West Perspective," *Novuum Testamentum,* vol. 35 (2003): 311-348.

ethnocentrism assumes a different form. Though, there are occasions where socialization does take place, by and large the social relationship is marked by subtle tension. For example, ignorance about the region and caste consciousness result in a condescending attitude by people of mainland India towards ethnic groups of Northeast India whereas suspicion of the stranger, the feeling of insecurity against probable onslaught and domination by outsiders and dislike for a culture and religion which stand in contrast to what is their own make the people of Northeast India to disassociate from forging social relationship with people from mainland India. Though, ethnocentric behaviour and attitudes is evident in both sides since one considers the language, culture and lifestyle of the other as odd and inferior to what is their own, it should be noted that in the context of Northeast India, ethnocentrism is more intensely expressed and manifested by the people of Northeast India.

In the context of the different group of people in Northeast India, ethnocentrism is a destructive force to be reckoned with because Northeast India in itself is as diverse as India. In addition to that social interaction between the diverse groups also takes place almost every day. The intensity of ethnocentrism in Northeast India is evident in the frequent incidents of ethnic conflicts which have torn the region from the 1990s till today. But even in those situations which have not witnessed any bloodshed or violence, conflicts exist in subtle and covert forms such as expression of condescending attitudes towards others groups, disassociation and isolation of the weaker group from sharing power and resources and so on. For example, groups which are more advanced economically and in terms of literacy like the Khasi, the Aos, and the Lushais tend to look down and isolate their neighbouring groups. In the process, the other groups at the receiving end would counteract thereby resulting in an atmosphere of friction and conflict. It may be significant to mention here that ethnocentric attitude and behaviour is one of the reasons for the inability of different groups in the Northeast to come together for a meaningful purpose be it in the political, the religious or the social sphere. Therefore, ethnocentrism is a destructive force in the context of the different group of people in Northeast India.

Hence, ethnocentrism in the context of Northeast India, as an unhealthy attitude and behaviour towards others, works at two levels, namely, the people of Northeast India having a negative attitude towards those from mainland India, and a particular group having negative attitude towards a neighbouring group or another group from the region itself.

Paul's Response to Ethnocentrism and Its Implication in the Context of Northeast India

Jews, Greeks and barbarians are significant social markers in the social world of Pauline Christianity because they mirror the problem of ethnocentrism. However, an analysis of the use of these terms in Rom 1:14, 16 shows that ethnocentrism is being challenged at in the Pauline Churches and communities. Paul's response to the problem of ethnocentrism is not by radically subverting the identities, positions and status occupied by these groups but by acknowledging the contributions of the other or the outsiders in the propagation of the gospel and by incorporating and integrating different and groups in conflict into the assembly of the early Christian communities. This is clearly evident in Paul's expression of indebtedness to the Greek and barbarians who are the other or outsiders to his mission work (Rom 1:14). In addition to that, Paul also tries to incorporate and transform groups like Jews and Greeks into a community.

In the wider framework of the Pauline writings, it may be reminded that bias and prejudice based on ethnicity, class, status, and gender are abrogated (Rom 10:12; Gal 3:27-28; 1 Cor 12:12-13). In fact, the communities which can be visualized in the Pauline writings can be taken as models of an ideal church where the various social factors which promote and enhance ethnocentrism are kept in control. Here, it may be mentioned that Paul does not negate the identity of any social group as evident in his use of terms (like Jews, Greek, barbarians, men, women, slaves, free and so on).[26] And neither does he promote and escalate that identity so as to become ethnocentric. As such, the use of the terms Jews, Greeks and

26 However, it may be noted that some terms like barbarians and slaves have negative connotations.

barbarians in Rom 1:14, 16 further strengthen the Pauline theology and mission of building inclusive communities.

In the fragile context of Northeast India where the ethnic factor plays an important role in dividing people and destroying communities, Paul's response to ethnocentrism assumes importance. Paul acknowledges the presence of a mild and moderate dose of ethnocentrism by not negating social identity but he counters and reacts against excess and overt ethnocentrism with theological statements which abrogate bias and prejudice based on social factors like ethnicity, class and gender. Indeed, Paul does not react with aggression or with any radical or revolutionary subversion but he does so by rationalizing the entire process of accommodating and integrating people and communities. For instance, he acknowledges where acknowledgment is due and he tries to bring people together. Drawing from this Pauline paradigm, it is a must for the people of Northeast India to mutually show recognition and respect for the other instead of showing attitudes; the contribution of the other should also be mutually acknowledged; and creating inclusive communities and coming together for a meaningful purpose should also be strived.

Conclusion

In many societies both past and present, overt ethnocentrism is a behaviour and attitude which divide people and communities. The various groups within the social world of Pauline communities and the different social groups in Northeast India were deeply affected by ethnocentrism. However, the references to Jews, Greeks and barbarians in Rom 1:14, 16 show that Paul responded to this divisive factor by acknowledging their identities, their importance and their contributions to the propagation of the gospel. Indeed, Paul tried to incorporate and integrate the different groups within the early Christian communities as one community. Hence, Paul's response to ethnocentrism assumes significance and importance to the world at large and to the churches in Northeast India in particular.

3

Racism
Perspectives from the Tribal Customs and Practices

Hukato N. Shohe[1]

"Racism has historically been a banner to justify the enterprises of expansion, conquest, colonization and domination and has walked hand in hand with intolerance, injustice and violence."
- Rigoberta Mench Tum, Guatemalan Indigenous Leader and Nobel Peace Prize Laureate

In a world of rapid change and globalization, encounter of one group with the other, hitherto relatively isolated, is the norm. Parochial and provincial existence, isolated and segregated from the rest of the world is no longer an option. This encounter or meeting of the diverse groups has both negative and positive aspects. Positively it widens the world horizon, opportunities, choices or possibilities. Nonetheless, because of the limitations in resources, unequal power equations or unequal relational equations, differences arises among the groups with regard to sharing of resources, power, opportunities, etc. Within this reality, an attempt is made to retrace some aspects of traditional tribal costumes and practices and its implication against Racism or Racial discrimination.

---

1 Dr. Hukato N. Shohe is the Academic Dean at the Trinity Theological College, Dimapur, Nagaland.

Term and Meaning

Racism is the belief that apparent differences between groups results in different levels of capacity and ability thereby justifying discrimination. This distinction and classification at one point of time claimed scientific basis for the theory. Fortunately, as Jonathan Marks states, "...vast majority of ideas that most scientist have ever had have been wrong" even more importantly he also points out that "the pronouncements of scientist on human variations may be loaded with cultural prejudices...and as history shows us, indeed they have usually been...Except that, as pronouncements of scientist, these ultimately cultural values would subsequently be vested with the authority of science. The culture can consequently produce the values that the scientist validates, thus, proving that the culture was right all along."[2]

The *Oxford English Dictionary (1936) defines the term* as "[t] he theory that distinctive human characteristics and abilities are determined by race." Additionally, the OED records *racism* as a synonym of *racialism*: "belief in the superiority of a particular race." Racism, in its simplest and rather naïve meaning would be to understand that human beings are divided in separate races accounting for the difference in colour or appearances and these external differences or appearances indicates the difference in intellectual ability and capacity. Such perception of humans as being neatly classified under three or four blocks of types now longer holds water. Today, most biologists, anthropologists, and sociologists reject the racial classification in favor of more specific and/or empirically verifiable criteria, such as geography, ethnicity, or a history of endogamy.[3]

2 Jonathan Marks, Bio-Diversity-Genes, Race and History (New Brunswick: n.p., 2009), p. 2.

3 "...the attempt to depict variations in terms of 'sub-species' or 'races' ...were doomed to failure biologically...It was the growing perception that cases such as this represent the norm for the biological world that led to the realization that the presumed existence of units such as 'sub-species'-or 'races' in the human realm-derived more from traditions of medieval theology than from assessment of how the biological world is actually put together. The demonstration that such a concept does more harm than good in the everyday business of trying to

Kuldeep Singh[4] states that "Racism and Racial discrimination are often used to describe discrimination on an ethnic or cultural basis, independent of their somatic differences. Similarly, while the UN does not define "racism;" it does define "racial discrimination" without any distinction between race, ethnic, national or cultural discrimination. It states,

> the term "racial discrimination" shall mean any distinction, exclusion, restriction, or preference based on race, colour, descent, or national or ethnic origin that has the purpose or effect of nullifying or impairing the recognition, enjoyment or exercise, on an equal footing, of human rights and fundamental freedoms in the political, economic, social, cultural or any other field of public life.[5]

In this definition *Racism* and *racial discrimination* are used synonymously, no distinction is made between discrimination based on ethnicity and race, in part because the distinction between the two remains debatable among anthropologists. Similarly, in British law the phrase *racial group* means "any group of people who are defined by reference to their race, colour, nationality (including citizenship) or ethnic or national origin." In Norway, the word "race" has been removed from national laws concerning discrimination as the use of the phrase is considered problematic and unethical. The Norwegian

---

make sense out of variation in ordinary biological species was first articulated by E. O. Wilson, ...famous for his promotion of *Sociobiology.*" Ashley Montagu, *Man's Most Dangerous Myth: The Fallacy of Race*, Walnut Creek: Alta Mira Press, 1997, p-xx. Ref. for biology, E. O. Wilson, *Socio-biology: The New Synthesis* (Cambridge: Belknap Press, 1975.; for Genetics, Joseph B. Birdsell, "Some Implications of the Genetical Concept of Race in Terms of Spatial Analysis," *Proceedings of the Cold Spring Harbour Symposia on Quantitative Biology* 15 (1951), 259-311. For bloodline, Frank B. Livingstone, "Anthropological Implications of Sickle Cell Gene Distribution in West Africa" The American Anthropologist. 30 (3) (1958), 533-562.

4 Kuldeep Singh, *Human Rights and Social Justice*. New Delhi: Sonali Publications, 2012, 117.

5 "International Convention on the Elimination of All Forms of Racial Discrimination." Office of the United Nations High Commissioner for Human Rights. Retrieved December 23, 2011.

Anti-Discrimination Act bans discrimination based on ethnicity, national origin, descent and skin color.

From the above discussion on the meaning of Racism, three implications of societal significance can be discerned. Namely,

> The belief that each race has distinct and intrinsic attributes.
> This distinct attribute indicates the capacity and development of each race or group.
> This varying capacity and development is the rationale for discrimination.

Nature of Racial Discrimination

The term Racism or Racial Discrimination by its very meaning implies the presence of the other since it is based on the notion of distinction from the other. As such, two aspects of racial discrimination that forms its basis are as follow:

Racism or Racial discrimination is relational[6]- it occurs within the context of encounter with the other-the majority with the minority, the more educated with the less educated, etc.

Thus, in a changed scenario the discriminated one may become the discriminator, when the status of the group/s or community/ies changes from being the dominant to subordinate or vice-versa, or the subordinate assumes the position of the dominant. For instance, with the retreat of the colonial powers, the dominated nationals who became the dominant group were and are accused of discriminatory policies.

Therefore, racism or racial discrimination is more complex than it appears and set within the perspective of relation. Thus, to understand racism one must deal with the question of the meaning of race and the various cognates – such as nationalism, ethnicism,

---

6 "Nationalism may be emancipator in relation to colonialism and external domination but turns into domination when it takes the form of internal colonialism, xenophobia, and chauvinism, imposes a monocultural regime and practices suppression and discrimination of minorities and deliberate uneven development across regions." States Jan Nederveen Pieterse, in "Ethnicities and Multiculturalism: Politics of Boundaries" in *Ethnicities, Nationalism and Minority Rights*. Eds. Stephen May, Tariq Modood and Judith Squires (Cambridge: Cambridge University Press, 2004), pp. 27-49.

cultural jingoism, etc., understood within context, among others, of the broad definition of Racial Discrimination set in the International Convention on the Elimination of All Forms of Racial Discrimination (ICEFRD) of the UN.

Secondly, like ethnicity, racism or racial discrimination must be seen and understood within the context of relationships.[7] History points to the fact that discrimination occurs within the vortex of power and resource. Thus, discrimination occurs where there is short supply of the later, or need to control is felt. Though, in reality the two always goes hand in hand, since power and resource, are for all practical reasons, corollary to one another, one perpetuating and undergirding the other. As Ernie Regeher rightly observes, "While almost two-thirds of the armed conflicts in 1992 could have been defined as conflicts of ethnicity, this should not be confused with identifying the causes of these conflicts. Behind ethnic or national identity struggles are basic economic and social grievances that need to be redressed."[8]

Lewis Coser, defines social conflict as '... a struggle over the values and claims to scarce status, power and resources in which the aims of the opponents are to neutralize, injure, or eliminate their rivals.'[9] In other words, discrimination is the consequence of the struggle between two or more groups in their quest to control, where the dominant group resorts to unfair and unjust means to dominate over the others by means of ignoring or depreciating the others right to equal and just opportunity, resources and control.

In addition to the struggle for control is the tendency of dominant groups to subsume the subordinate groups within its fold. This causes resentment and suspicion and serves a fuel for conflict. As Miroslav Volf observes, "...this pattern of debasement

---

7 D. Dewyer and S. R. Drakakis (eds.) *Ethnicity and Development: Geographical Perspectives* (Chichester: Wiley), 1996, p. 4.

8 Ernie Regehr. "Armed Conflict in the World in 1992: A World Made Safe from War?" *Ploughshares Monitor* 13, 4 (1992): 17. Cited in A Moment to Choose: Risking to be with Uprooted People - A Resource book (WCC, 1996), p. 90.

9 Lewis Coser, *The Functions of Social Conflict* (New York: The Free Press), 1956. cited in "Social conflict" *Wikipedia*, https://en.wikipedia.org/wiki/Social_conflict. 3/11/2015, 03:15 PM.

is being repeated today in many parts of the world: the 'others' are first dehumanized or demonized and then discriminated against, marginalized, driven out or destroyed."[10]

History speaks to this, where in post-Renaissance and post-French Revolution European history, the idea of the nation and the state being considered identical within politically sovereign territorial boundaries developed with its idea of equating the modern state with a single nation. Consequently, smaller communities, ethnic or religious or racial, were basically over-run by the dominant groups or more powerful nations. Some of these smaller nations disappeared; others were absorbed into the larger national entities. "In the contemporary world this process has been going on for some time, and it has created new challenges for the smaller communities who call themselves either ethnic groups or racial groups or distinct communities. These small nations do not like the idea of being hegemonized or absorbed into the larger entities of what is called the nation, particularly in the non-European world."[11] Thus, blatant cultural hegemony creates an atmosphere of fear leading to further need to preserve or resurging identities on perceived threatened ethnic lines. Thus, resentment and discrimination may develop at the micro-level as a defense mechanism against the dominant group's hegemonic tendency. It is within this context that one needs to understand the Traditional Customary law and practice of the tribals and the changes taking place in contemporary tribal or indigenous society.

Traditional Tribal Societies and Racial Discrimination[12]

The traditional Naga tribal context have been portrayed as being isolated from the others, nonetheless, this must not be construed

10 Miroslav Volf, "A Vision of Embrace: Theological Perspectives on Cultural Identity and Conflict." *The Ecumenical Review. The Ecumenical Review* 47, 2 (1995): 195.

11 Jaradeva Uyangoda. "Understanding Ethnicity and Nationalism." *The Ecumenical Review* 47, 2 (1995): 190.

12 The following section is based on my interviews with some people from different communities. The findings does not claim to represent all tribal costumes or practices, since the interaction was limited to a small group.

as living in total isolation away from the others. Naga history is replete with contact, friendship and conflict among the various Naga tribes, with other non-Naga neighbours like Ahoms, Meities, tribes in Arunachal, etc. Thus, there was some contact and interaction with the outside world, the village polity as a society was generally isolated from the outside influence, atleast major, allowing the Nagas to develop their own cultures and way of life.

The Significance of Traditional Culture

Culture is a complex term that seeks to explain or represent the total response of a community to the environment. Culture is broadly defined by George Lobo as the "way of life of a people, the commonly accepted aims and assumptions on which habits, ways of thought and expressions are based, including values and beliefs."[13] Unlike the oft misused meaning, referring to certain high culture as in taste and approval of the elite, culture than is much more than taste in music, literature or such like. It is the very pattern of life that emerges in a society in response to the internal and external factors. Somen Das refers to three aspects of a culture which embraces all the individual and community life namely the ideational, materiality and experiential.[14] It includes the pattern of thinking and participation as much as the recollection of history and living out the values and beliefs.[15] Culture marks each society as distinct from the other.

Into this pre-set world is a person born into, socialized and conscientized into its peculiar forms of action and responses, modes of thinking-worldview, ideology, patterns of behavior ideals and belief. It is not a surprise that anthropologists consider culture "stronger than life and stronger than death ...but culture triumphs

13 George Lobo, "The Church and Neo-colonialism" D. S. Amalopavordoss, ed. *The Indian Church in the Struggle for a New Society* (Bangalore, 1981), 240.

14 Somen Das, *Christian Faith in Multi-faith Culture in India* (Bangalore: UTC, 1987), p. 4.

15 Cf. Sathianathan Clarke, "Exploration of Intercultural Theological Methodologies in Asia" in *Inter-Cultural Theological Methodologies: An Exploration*. Ed. Samson Prabhakar. (Bangalore: South Asian Theological Research Institute, 202), 4-7.

over death and offers man eternal life."[16] Thus, hegemonic threat of assimilation or attempt to subsuming of the Naga or other tribal society also needs to be taken into consideration to understand the prevailing condition, not only of the Naga tribes, but with regard to most of the indigenous tribes in India.

The case of the Naga tribal communities would point to such an encounter. While there is much visible change undertaking in the Naga context, which may appear to be normal at the surface level. The suppressed feelings of inadequacies and incompleteness are but revealed in the conflict and restlessness erupting in violence within itself and with the others. Nonetheless, there is also a sense of continuity with the traditional society, that acts both as a point of reference against the changes as well as the model for change which may actually be the result of selective amnesia.[17]

Within the context of seclusion the Cultural world of the tribals, the traditional customary laws and practices pertaining to racism or racial discrimination needs to be understood. While customary laws may or may not have been fossilized into written documents, the nearness of the past practices, particularly some practices or institutions, may have some implications to understand the traditional customary laws towards racism. With this in mind, the following areas are touched upon for our purpose:

The Practice of Adoption

Without going into the details, it will suffice to point out that the practice of adoption was practiced among the Nagas. Adoption may take place under any or various reasons either personal or for social obligations. In the course of my conversation with various people either elders, or those socially concerned or experts in the customary practices, it was observed that while the Naga traditional societies were strongly communitarian, room for individuality was ample, where the individual choices and/or decision/s was/were respected

16 Ludwig Beiler and Michael Schattenhoffer, "The Concepts and Components of Culture" in *The New Encyclopaedia Britannica,* Vol. 16 Macropaedia. 15 Edition. (Chicago: Encyclopaedia Britannica, Inc, 1986), 927.

17 B. Kuppuswamy, *Social Change in India* (New Delhi: Vikas Publishing House Pvt. Ltd., 1989), 3.

by the community, as long as these did not infringe on the customs or practices. Thus, for any reason a person may be adopted- prisoners of war, aliens seeking shelter in the village, orphans, those meeting dire economic situations, etc.

When a person is adopted into a family, the adoptee was usually inducted into the family and clan of the adopter. The adopted person becomes one of the family members and by extension a member of the clan and the village, the apex social unit of the tribals. Once a person is adopted into the family all familial obligations and responsibilities were invested upon the adopted.

It may be noted that there was no law/custom or practice that denied the adoptee from becoming a part of the adopters family, in every sense of the word. However, it is also to be noted that the treatment of the adoptee was solely at the discretion of the adopter. Hence, while some of the adoptee were treated as any members of the family by bloodline, in some cases the adoptee were denied some privileges. Secondly, such treatments were equally meted out to both adoptees from or outside of the village, tribe or others. In other words, denial of privileges was extended not on the basis of the who or where the adoptee originated from, but on the basis of the individual whim of the adopter.

Socio-Cultural Life

The life of the village-state and the tribal community were a cohesive unit, each participating in the whole, and the whole providing the rationale and meaning for the individual. The question of whether alternative cultural practice, however, does not arise in the traditional tribal set-up. The above reason being one. The reason may be because of the nature of the traditional socio-political set-up where in such an encounter did not arise.

Certainly, no example of the non-tribal neighbors of the Nagas coming to settle among the Nagas with their cultural practices and religion could be traced in my short interaction with the interviewees. At the most was the case of adoption of others. As such, no direct reference can be made as to whether the tribal communities discriminated against other cultural practice. As a tribal and in my various interactions for this and others, the nearest cultural discriminatory attitude, if it may be called so, is "that is their way," "that is others' way," or such like. Usually a value free comment recognizing the otherness of the other.

If one may pursue through indirect means, however, one can have some approximate estimate of what would be the attitude if such a case arose. However, this is merely a conjectural deduction and reality may actually have been a contrasting reaction. Nonetheless, the alternative practices[18] within the tribal communities like the lycanthropy and their acceptance may point towards the possibility of a more tolerant attitude.

Economy and Livelihood

The traditional economy was subsistence economy based on land and its products. The chief economic occupation was cultivation. Every family had number of lands for cultivation. Generally, the head of the family or clan distributed the land for cultivation amongst the family members. Every family was entitled to land for cultivation, as such the adoptees were also given a plot of land for cultivation.

As mentioned in the preceding section, no customary practice or law existed that barred the extension of this entitlement to the adoptee. Thus, each member of the family were provided with equal opportunity to better their economic condition. Of course, individual treatment varied from person to person. It is worth noting that, regardless of individual disposition, social obligation and social status demanded that everyone be given a share in land distribution for cultivation. This social obligation and standing[19] was one mechanism that ensured economic and livelihood security.

Thus, economic discrimination, if anything was foreign to the life and community of the tribals, if not for any other reason, the availability of land, the nature of subsistence economy based on ones' willingness to work and communitarian spirit ensured that no one

18 Strictly speaking these were not alternative culture or society but they were not the norm, these people represented differentness, other practice.

19 A word or two is in order to understand the importance of social obligation and status of the tribals. As a communitarian society, the highest recognition and achievement of every individual was social standing. This is based on ones' acceptance of ones' social obligations and responsibilities.

is discriminated against economically. Leave alone an adoptee, even a serf[20] who has no land to cultivate brings into question the very ability and social responsibility of the patron or the adopter. This would result in the almost irreparable loss of standing and prestige of the adopter in the community, and with it all other social privileges and responsibilities.

Decision making and Political Structure

Traditionally, every village was an independent unit- no obligation or requirement, to any other village for making decisions pertaining to war or any other policy. In modern terms every village was a sovereign, independent state, solely dependent on its own resources and capacity to make decisions and execute them. Such decision was arrived at through discussion and strategy arrived at by the council.

The council members were constituted by the elders and capable & prominent members of the village along with the king or chief or some similar head. It is interesting to note that, even in such a council, the highest decision making body, regardless of whether a person was adopted or member by biology, were selected to be a part and parcel of the body, if capable and fit. The exception in this case being an adoptee who was adopted as an adult, or someone who had come of age in understanding when adopted.

While the adult adoptee may not be included in the highest decision making body, the adoptee's offspring, if capable were inducted into this council. This exclusion can be compared with any modern nation-states where the head of the state or members of the highest decision making bodies are expected to be citizens of a nation or state by birth. This is not surprising in that the security and life of the nation-state or village – state depends on this body and any possible preemption of betrayals and treason must be taken into

20 Serf is the word I use to refer to the practice of Aqü-axe among the Sumi people, where in a person is for various reason obligated to live under a patron. Some have used the word slave to interpret this institution, however, the practice of aqü-axe and slave as practiced in the occidental world are entirely different where the rights and responsibilities do not match, except for the fact that an aqü-axe is tied to the patron, though he/she may buy her freedom when and if the aqü-axe so desires and have the capacity, the price for which can be very high.

consideration. Thus, discrimination on the basis or any attributes, colour, skin, hair, etc., was not known or insignificant. What marks the tribal society is their acceptance of an individual on the basis of their ability and trustworthiness.

The Contemporary Problem in Racial Discrimination

Discrimination arises out of scarcity of resources and the need to control the resources. The contemporary tribal society, like any other societies, face scarcity of resources and stiff competition for control among themselves and from the others. It is in this context that there is a need to ponder on the issue of discrimination. Whatever be the case, the traditional practice and laws may not provide any basis for upholding any form of discrimination.

The recent for job reservation for "Nagas by blood" is certainly a call for preserving whatever little resources for the indigenous people of Nagaland. Job reservation is a demand not peculiar to the state of Nagaland. Every state in India has reservation for the citizens of the state. In this case, it would be wrong to forget the "Sons of the Soil" movement in the larger and more advanced states of India.[21]

However, we also need to ponder on the issue of "by blood" since the rationale behind this must be that the Nagas are pure breed and no dilution have taken place with other non-Nagas. What is the basis for such a demand? What of the adopted people who have become Nagas in every sense of the word, except for their biological connection in the past of which they are not aware.[22]Are we contradicting the very thing we claim to fight for- the traditional individual right to adopt one chooses to? The traditional costumes which had no room for racial discrimination? Perhaps, more room for discussion is required, whatever be the case discussion must commence least we throw the baby with the bathwater.

---

21 Some well known cases are Maharashtra's MNS and Shiv Sena party (1966), Anti-Hindi agitation of Tamilnadu, and Assam's 1961's expulsion of Bengalis, etc.

22 Refer above Term and Meaning, and Footnote 2.

Bibliography

Amalopavordoss, D.S., ed. *The Indian Church in the Struggle for a New Society*. Bangalore, (n.p.), 1981.

Coser, Lewis *The Functions of Social Conflict*. New York: The Free Press, 1956.

Das, Somen *Christian Faith in Multi-faith Culture in India*. Bangalore: UTC, 1987. Dewyer, D. and S. R. *Ethnicity and Development: Geographical Perspectives*. Chichester: Wiley, Drakakis (eds.), 1996.

Kuppuswamy, B. *Social Change in India*. New Delhi: Vikas Publishing House Pvt. Ltd., 1989.

Marks, Jonathan *Bio-Diversity-Genes, Race and History*. New Brunswick: n.p., 2009.

May, Stephen, Tariq Modood and Judith Squires, eds. *Ethnicities, Nationalism and Minority Rights*. Cambridge: Cambridge University Press, 2004.

Montagu, Ashley *Man's Most Dangerous Myth: The Fallacy of Race*. Walnut Creek: Alta Mira Press, 1997.

Prabhakar, Samson Ed. *Inter-Cultural Theological Methodologies: An Exploration*. Bangalore: SATHRI, 2002.

Singh, Kuldeep *Human Rights and Social Justice*. New Delhi: Sonali Publications, 2012.

Wilson, E. O. *Socio-biology: The New Synthesis*. Cambridge: Belknap Press, 1975.

Journals, Documents, etc.

A Moment to Choose: Risking to be with Uprooted People - A Resource Book (WCC, 1996).

"International Convention on the Elimination of All Forms of Racial Discrimination." Office of the United Nations High Commissioner for Human Rights. Retrieved December 23, 2011.

Ploughshares Monitor 13, 4 (1992).

Proceedings of the Cold Spring Harbour Symposia on Quantitative Biology 15 (1951), 259-311.

The American Anthropologist. 30, (3) (1958), 533-562.

The Ecumenical Review 47, 2 (1995).

The New Encyclopaedia Britannica, Vol. 16 Macropaedia. 15 Edition. (1986).

Interviewees

Dr. Nokching Chollen, Traditional/Alternative Medicine Practitioner, Eralibil.

Prof. Mufotiba Longkumer, Dimapur Govt. College, Notun Basti, Dimapur.

Rev. Thilihe Yeptho, Church Worker, 87 yrs, Thahekhu.

Rev. Yanbemo, Pastor LBC, Dimapur.

Rev. Tonlong Konyak, Pastor, Former ES., KBBES, Dimapur.

Mr. Kakheto Sema, Addl. Adv. Gen., Dimapur.

4

Racism and Religion (Christianity)
An Ethical Reading

Shimreingam L. Shimray[1]

Racism is almost as old as the human race. It appears in many forms, both crude and subtle. Racism exists when we allow color, caste, language, nationality, tribe, ethnicity, culture or any such factor to erect a wall between people either individually or corporately so that one exercises contempt, prejudice, or lordship over another.[2] It is clearly understandable if you know why caste system did not die even after the legal burial in India. Caste system is no doubt very destructive and harmful but those people who maintain caste system do it not because they are inhuman but because they are too religious. Those people who follow this racial religion may not, however, admit that they adhere to religion of their own. Nevertheless, racism shares all the essential characteristics of religion, secular or supernatural.[3] As a religion, racism offers a sense of power. Racists make the superior race the center of value and the object of devotion. Therefore, in this

1 Rev. Dr. Shimreingam L. Shimray is Professor and Head of the Department of Christian Ethics and Social Analysis at the Eastern Theological College, Jorhat, Assam.

2 Samuel Koranteng-Pipim, "Religion versus Christianity" in *Dialogue – An International Journal of Faith, Thought and Action.*

3 Elizabeth K. Nottingham, *Religion and Society* (New York: Random House, 1954), 1-11.

religion, members find their sense and "power of being" from their membership in and identification with the superior race. Racism's power takes two major forms: legal racism in which discriminatory practices are encoded in the laws of the land (apartheid, Nazism, slavery); and institutional racism where racial practices, even without the benefit of law, are subtly built into various social structures.[4]

Defining the Term

The Human Rights and Equal Opportunity Commission in Australia (1998) defines it as:

> "Racism is an ideology that gives expression to myths about other racial and ethnic groups that devalues and renders inferior those groups that reflects and is perpetuated by deeply rooted historical, social, cultural and power inequalities in society."
>
> Anthropologist Ruth Benedict points out that racism is a religion that is established on a naturalistic worldview. Racism, she states, is "the dogma that one ethnic group is condemned by Nature to hereditary inferiority and another group is destined to hereditary superiority. It is the dogma that the hope of civilization depends upon eliminating some races and keeping others pure."[5]

Racism is destructive. It disempowers people by devaluing their racial identity. It destroys community cohesion and creates divisions in society. It is the opposite of the democratic principle of equality and the right of all people to be treated fairly. Thus, the definition of racism may be summed up by referring to the 1965 U.N. Convention which expressed its conviction on racism forcefully: "Any doctrine of superiority based on the difference between races is scientifically false, morally condemnable and socially unjust and dangerous."[6]

Racism has its roots in the belief that some people are superior because they belong to a particular race, ethnic or national group. The

---

4 Samuel Koranteng-Pipim, "Religion versus Christianity."

5 Ruth Benedict, *Race: Science and Politics* (New York: Viking Press, 1959), 98.

6 Par. 6 of the Preamble of the International Convention on the Elimination of All Forms of Racial Discrimination, which was adopted on December 21, 1965, and which entered into force on January 4, 1969.

concept of race is a social construct, not a scientific one. Racism is the result of a complex interplay of individual attitudes, social values and institutional practices. It is expressed in the actions of individuals and institutions and is promoted in the ideology of popular culture. Examples of racist behaviour include ridicule, racist abuse, property damage, racial harassment, racist propaganda, racial vilification and physical assault. It also includes practices that exploit or exclude members of particular groups from aspects of society.[7] This form of racism reflects the cultural assumptions of the dominant group, so that the practices of that group are seen as the norm to which other cultural practices should conform. Take example of banning meat in parts of India during the Jain festival of Paryushan on 13 and 18 September 2015.[8] It regularly and systematically advantages some ethnic and cultural groups and disadvantages and marginalizes others. Imbedded in the very definition is the erroneous view that there are various human races. That is not a convincing way of reading the principle of God's creation. There is only one race—the human race! We come in different sizes, shapes, colors, etc.... but we are essentially the same, human. Racism stems from the sinful notions that some colors are better than others, that some cultures are better than others that some physical features are better than others, or that one gender is better than the other.[9] Racism is not always obvious, and that is part of its danger. It can have many different forms and it is usually less extreme than the examples printed in textbooks. The different levels of racism are so dangerous because they can easily hide in society. One of the famous political activists in America, Angela Davis, said it best: "Racism is a much more clandestine, much more hidden kind of phenomenon, but at the same time it's perhaps far

7 http.www.racismnoway.com.au/about-racism/understanding/culture-language-identity.html./1209/2015

8 Even if the claim was made on slaughter of animal that was an attempt to cover up because the issue does not lie on it. Cf. The Bombay High Court's question was valid when it asked 'if the ban is on slaughter why then only on mutton and chicken and not on fish and egg?' *The Telegraph*, Guwahati September 15, 2015.

9 Juan Valdes, "Racism: Christian Perspective" Posted on July 26, 2013 by Reasons for Hope / http://www..rforh.com/uncategorized/red-and-yellow-black-and-white-a-christian-perspective-onracism/#sthash.xVt5LZmJ.dpuf

more terrible than it's ever been."[10] This is a dangerous concept to deal with humanity who are equally created in the image of God.

Trevor J. Major and Richard D. Melson made an explicit explanation on the nature of racism when they wrote about two forms of racism. Racism may take two forms, with people sometimes harboring one, or both, varieties. (1) **Condescending racism** is where a person lessens the status of another group. Such a person may regard people of another race as simple, child-like creatures with lazy work habits, deficient intelligence, superstitious minds, and/or questionable morals. (2) **Competitive racism** occurs when one group fears competition with another group (e.g., when a new group moves into a community and competes with the existing population for jobs and housing). The difference is the starting point: condescending racism begins with the assumption that a certain race is inherently inferior; competitive racism begins with a fear of another race.[11]

Institutional racism is often the most difficult to recognize and counter, particularly when it is perpetrated by institutions and governments who do not view themselves as racist. When present in a range of social contexts, this form of racism reinforces the disadvantage already experienced by some members of the community. For example, racism experienced by students at school may result in early school dropout and lower educational outcomes. Together with discrimination in employment, this may lead to fewer employment opportunities and higher levels of unemployment for these students when they leave school. In turn, lower income levels combined with discrimination in the provision of goods and services restrict access to housing, health care and life opportunities generally. In this way, institutional racism may be particularly damaging for minority groups and further restrict their access to services and participation in society.

10 Quoted by Jasmine Anderson, "Breaking the Barrier: Racism" in *Ethos* (Volume 2013 [*Fall 2013*]), 2.

11 Trevor J. Major and Richard D. Melson, *A Christian Response to Racism* (Montgomery: Apologetic Press, Inc.), 1994, 2.

Racial Imposition and Contradiction

How did the racism intruded into the Christian Church and nurtured to become a force that would create space for the non-coloured people in the West needs to understand from their interpretation of the "image of God." Karen Teel, in her book, *Racism and the Image of God* exposed that the Western Christianity has traditionally taught that the soul or mind best represents God's image in humans; in the United States bodily differences, especially those often labeled "racial," have been used to justify hierarchies of worth. Karen Teel argues that bodies deserve respect as part of the image of God. This is a crucial aspect because it threatens even the universal position of defining equality.[12]

The Church of Jesus Christ of Latter-day Saints also took harsh position on blacks and the priesthood. Blacks have been members of the LDS Church since the 1830s. However, on the basis of their interpretation of a passage prohibited the blacks. They believed that the mark that Cain received after killing Abel was dark skin (blacks). In 1848, church prophet and President Brigham Young declared that descendants of Cain could not be ordained to the priesthood. This impacted blacks on every continent, not just slaves or freedmen in the United States.[13]

Josiah Priest quotes liberally from scripture, citing numerous examples of enslavement being sanctified in the Bible. He writes, "If God appointed the race of Ham judicially to slavery (Genesis 9:18-27), and it were a heinous sin to enslave one, or all the races, how then is the appointment of God to go into effect? .... God does never sanction sin, nor call for the commission of moral evil to forward any of his purposes; wherefore we come to the conclusion, that is not sinful to enslave the negro race, providing it is done in a tender, fatherly and thoughtful manner."[14] His interpretation was that "Ham [the son of Noah], he was 'cussed,' and so 'they' [the dark-

12 Karen Teel, *Racism and the Image of God* (Publishers: Palgrave Macmillan - Ebook (PDF), 2011.

13 Lynette Roberson, "Racism and the Church: Do We Demand Change?" in *The Huffington Post*, September 1, 2015.

14 Josiah Priest, *Bible Defence of Slavery: And Origin, Fortunes, and History of the Negro Race.*

skinned] are not as good as us." This white-racist "theology" has been all too prominent in American history — though it has no sanction at all in the Bible.[15]

Priest's interpretations of the Bible were particularly popular in the American South, with the Southern Baptists championing religious justifications for enslavement. Prominent Baptist minister Richard Furman helped polarize southern white Baptists to support the institution of slavery; he wrote to the governor of South Carolina explaining that "the right of holding slaves is clearly established in the Holy Scriptures;" he specifically cites the "Israelites [being] directed to purchase their bond-men and bond-maids of the Heathen nations; except they were of the Canaanites, for these were to be destroyed. And it is declared that the persons purchased were to be their 'bond-men forever;' and an 'inheritance for them and their children."[16] It was not until 1995's Southern Baptist Convention that the organization issued an apology for its former stance on slavery. Similar incident also took place a little later when in November 1999, Royce Money, president of Abilene Christian University (Texas), stood before a black audience and confessed the university's past sins of practicing discrimination. He apologized and asked for forgiveness.[17]

The Bible teaches that knowledge of truth and reality comes "from above:" from a revelation of God in Jesus and in the written Word (John 17:3; 2 Timothy 3:15-17). Racism, on the other hand, appeals to sources "from below," which assume the existence of an alleged superior race and incorporates various versions of ethnic pride. For example, white racism in the 19th century found a comfortable epistemological basis in Darwin's theory of the survival of the fittest. In that theory Europeans received confirmation that "they were the fittest

15 Wayne Jackson, *The Tragedy of Racism;* People who attempt to justify racism from this passage argue that Ham had black skin because his name means "hot sunburnt." They combine this information with the statement that Canaan (symbolizing descendants of Ham) was cursed to be a slave ("servant of servants") to his brothers, and thus conclude that God's chosen people have authority to subjugate or enslave blacks.

16 http://www.alternet.org/belief/how-religious-liberty-has-been-used-justify-racism-sexism-and-slavery-throughout-history/12/09/2015

17 https://www.christiancourier.com/articles/146-tragedy-of-racism-the / 27/08/2015

of all."[18] Racism's version of truth thus ignores or rejects the biblical assertion that all human beings, created in the image of God, have a capacity to understand, empathize, appreciate, and communicate with each other, irrespective of racial background. Rejecting biblical revelation, the racist looks to sociology, anthropology, history, and science to explain and to address racial problems. Racism may consult the Bible at times, but only to find support to its postures.[19] Racism rejects the biblical doctrine of humanity and appeals to genetic or biological determinism to prop up its racial assumptions.

The Christian ethic and the racist ethic are inevitably at odds. The former is based on the "*sanctity* of human life," arising from the doctrine of Creation. The Bible presents the Ten Commandments as the clearest norm for human conduct, and Jesus as the supreme example for humanity. Racism, however, upholds the "*quality*-of-human-life" doctrine, which suggests that the personhood of human beings is determined by their biological characteristics, with some people having only *relative* value.[20] I would like to underline that human superiority of value on the basis of colour is unjustifiable because the blacks have a stronger gene and they should rather be considered as superior. For instance, when an Afro-American man married with a white woman their children are most black in colour; the same is true when a black woman married with a white woman their children are black in colour which only proves that the blacks have a stronger gene and they are to be a higher race; if at all necessary to rationalize the matter.

But in the religion of racism, the superior race is the center of human history. The racist believes that it is only "one race [the superior race that] has carried progress throughout human history and can alone ensure future progress."[21] Thus the racist not only

---

18 Alan Burns, *Colour Prejudice* (London: George Allen and Unwin Ltd., 1948), 23; cited in T. B. Maston, *The Bible and Race* (Nashville, Tenn.: Broadman Press, 1959), 64.

19 T. B. Maston, *The Bible and Race* (Nashville: Broadman Press, 1959), 105ff.

20 Joseph Fletcher, *Humanhood: Essays in Biomedical Ethics* (Buffalo, N.Y.: Prometheus, 1979), 12-18.

21 Ruth Benedict, *Race: Science and Politics* (New York: Viking Press, 1959), 98.

ignores, discounts, or distorts the histories of other races, but also refuses to listen to or learn from other races.[22]

It was subtle racism like this that colored the Religious Right's image in the 1980s. By the 1990s, it was getting harder to deny. Those outside the political arena began to call for "racial reconciliation" as a means of changing this perception. Groups such as Promise Keepers emphatically called upon white Christians to acknowledge their own prejudice and bridge the gap between their communities and those of color. But even such high profile groups drew skepticism and scorn from those who saw the brief pop in racial justice advocacy as a mere stunt. Proponents of the movement were simply paying lip service to the issue, so the argument went, and it certainly did seem like many were. "It doesn't translate into how you bring black and white together," says the Rev. Christopher M. Hamlin, pastor of the 16th Street Baptist Church in Birmingham, where a bombing by white segregationists killed four black children in 1963. "The barriers that are broken down in the stadiums are still there when people come home to their communities. I think most black pastors see it as being rhetoric, which is something most of the black community has heard for a long time."[23]

A racist position Theodore Bilbo had taken in the book, *Take Your Choice: Separation or Mongrelization* contributed towards developing racial hierarchy between the whites and the blacks he wrote, "Purity of race is a gift of God.... And God, in his infinite wisdom, has so ordained it that when man destroys his racial purity, it can never be redeemed," the concept has been echoed in several writings and speeches. Segregationist governor George Wallace invoked God 27 times in his famous speech that came to be known as "segregation now, segregation forever." Georgia governor Allen Candler said that "God made them negroes and we cannot by education make them white folks."[24]

22 Robert Hughes, *Culture of Complaint: The Fraying of America* (New York: Oxford University Press, 1993), 102.

23 (http://www.patheos.com/blogs/friendlyatheist/2015/06/29/the-religious-rights-racism-is-still-a-serious-problem-for-the-gop/) 19/8/2015

24 (http://www.alternet.org/belief/how-religious-liberty-has-been-used-justify-racism-sexism-and-slavery-throughout-history)

In all of these examples, religious belief is invoked to justify a right to discriminate. Proponents argue that constitutional protections for religious freedom are insufficient, and these new laws—aimed at granting businesses themselves exemptions from laws.[25]

Is Racism an Ethical Issue?

Racism is a serious ethical issue for the following reasons:

It denies the basic unity of the human family as the offspring of God. Adam and Eve are the grandparents of us all (Genesis 3:20).

The denigration of any human being, made in the image of God, is an assault upon the Creator himself (cf. Genesis 9:6). A human worth cannot be measured on the basis of colour of one's skin but his or her intrinsic being. Racism devalues the culture and lives of racial minorities. It also deprives the opportunity of the racial minorities. According to Billy Graham, racial and ethnic hatred is a sin, it is a sin precisely because it keeps us from obeying God's command to love our neighbor, and because it has its roots in pride and arrogance.[26]

It may also be noted that a secular argument against racism exists based on irrelevance of race as, (1) It is immoral to treat people differently for arbitrary reasons, and (2) treating people differently because of their race is arbitrary, since race is irrelevant to whether a person has certain technical abilities, rights, and benefits. (3) Therefore, racism is immoral.[27]

The first Biblical argument against racism is found in the Decalogue. The sixth commandment forbids us to take the life of another. Christ argues that the implications of this commandment are far deeper than simple murder. The Westminster Larger Catechism expounds the sixth commandment as forbidding, among other

25 (http://www.alternet.org/belief/how-religious-liberty-has-been-used-justify-racism-sexism-and-slavery-throughout-history)

26 Billy Graham, *THE ETHICS & RELIGIOUS LIBERTY COMISSION* of the Southern Baptist Convention, January 2010.

27 Douglas M. Jones III, "The Biblical Offense of Racism" cf. Spike Lee and Lisa Jones, *Do the Right Thing,* (New York; Simon and Schuster, 1989), 186, 187; Peter Singer, "Is Racial Discrimination Arbitrary?," in Jan Narveson, ed. *Moral Issue* (New York; Oxford University Press, 1983), 309.

things, "sinful anger, hatred, envy, desire of revenge...provoking words, oppression...striking, wounding, and whatsoever else tends to the destruction of the life of any". If we are forbidden to have or act on hateful attitudes toward anyone, then we are forbidden from doing such things to an individual of another race. Moreover, the Larger Catechism explains that the sixth commandment obligates us to preserve the life of others "by charitable thoughts, love, compassion, meekness, gentleness, kindness; peaceable, … ."[28]

The Christians believe that Christ died for all people (1 Timothy 2:5-6), any attempt to castigate a segment of humanity, suggesting its unworthiness, reflects upon the Savior's sacrifice. Divisive nature is no longer relevant in our highly civilized world. It has no rationale and needs to be discouraged.

If people and human communities are all equal in dignity, that does not mean that they all have, at a given moment, equal physical abilities, cultural endowments, intellectual and moral strengths, or that they are at the same stage of development. Equality does not mean uniformity. It is important to recognize the diversity and complementarity of one another's cultural riches and moral qualities. Equality of treatment therefore implies certain recognition of differences which minorities themselves demand in order to develop according to their own specific characteristics, in respect for others and for the common good of society and the world community. No human group, however, can boast of having a natural superiority over others, or of exercising any discrimination that affects the basic rights of the person.[29]

While religion, on the one hand, was and is used to support racial ideology and politics we see, on the other hand, religion (Christianity) as a source of inspiring and teaching tools to fight against racism. For instance, the experiences of Martin Luther King Jnr (1929-1968) and Archbishop Desmond Mpilo Tutu and Mother Teresa are excellent examples. Martin was born in 1929 and became

---

28 Douglas M. Jones III, "The Biblical Offense of Racism."

29 Cf. *Encyclical Pacem in Terris of John XXIII*, April 11, 1963, which denounces, following Pius XI, the scandal constituted by the persistence of ideologies according to which "some human beings or nations are superior to others by nature."

an accelerated student at Morehouse College at the age of fifteen, three years later he graduated with a BA degree in sociology and entered the Christian ministry because he believed this would give him a base from which to effect social change. He then went to Crozer Theological Seminary where he was influenced by the teaching of Mahatma Gandhi. He later said that from his background he gained his regulating Christian ideals and from Gandhi he learned his operational technique.[30] He led the black Americans towards Civil Rights with strong Christian principles.

Although, African-Americans transported to America as slaves had been freed when the Civil War ended in 1865 racism and segregation remained, especially in the southern states. As a boy Martin experienced racism and segregation in schools, restaurants and hospitals and on public transport and other public facilities. Many African-Americans were still denied the right to vote. In August 1963, 250,000 people marched to the Lincoln Memorial in Washington in solidarity with African-Americans and Dr. King delivered his *I have a dream* speech to the crowd. While he said, "I have a dream that one day this nation will rise up and live out the true meaning of its creed: We hold these truths to be self-evident: that all men are created equal."[31] One of his strongest questions was raised in relation to the condition of deprived workers in Memphis, Tennessee in 1968, which reads as,

> The question is not, 'If I stop to help this man in need, what will happen to me?' The question is, 'If I do not stop to help the sanitation workers, what will happen to them?' That's the question...

---

30 In 1955, he completed a doctorate in theology at Boston University and returned to Alabama where he became pastor of the Dexter Avenue Baptist Church in Montgomery. His church soon became a centre for social change. You may also see how Faith-Based Organizing works of Centre for Third World Organizing (CTWO), Pacific Institute for Community Organization (PICO) base at Oakland and Oakland Community Organization (OCO) during the 1990s that changed political democracy in America in *Faith in Action – Religion, race, and Democratic Organizing in America* edited by Richard L. Wood (Chicago and London: The University of Chicago Press, 2002).

31 Martin Luther King Jnr – "I have a dream", Speech delivered on the steps of the Lincoln Memorial in Washington DC 28 August, 1963.

> Like anybody, I would like to live a long life. Longevity has its place. But I'm not concerned about that now. I just want to do God's will, and He's allowed me to go up the mountain. And I've looked over and I've seen the Promised Land. I may not get there with you, but I want you to know tonight, that we as a people will get to the Promised Land.[32]

I am casually referring to Archbishop Desmond Mpilo Tutu in order to underline the religious contribution towards fighting against racism. He was one of the most effective activists against South African apartheid. He was born of Xhosa and Tswana parents at Klerksdorp in South Africa in 1931. He was educated in South African mission schools. His father was a respected schoolteacher but the family had little money and lived in a small shack without water or electricity. In 1936, the black South Africans' right to vote was abolished.

Although he wanted to be a doctor, Desmond was unable to afford medical school and instead became a schoolteacher. In 1955, the *Bantu Education Act*was passed which, in an effort to limit opportunity for black students, denied them maths and science instruction. In July of that year Desmond Tutu married Leah Nomalizo Shenxane. Together they have had four children. Desmond Tutu resigned from his teaching post in 1957, frustrated by the *Bantu Education Act.* In 1958, he began training for the Anglican priesthood. He said: "It just occurred to me that, if the Church would have me, the profession of priest could be a good way of serving my people."[33]

In 1978, Bishop Tutu became general secretary of the South African Council of Churches and a leading spokesperson for the rights of black South Africans. He emphasized peaceful means of protest and encouraged international economic sanctions against

32 On April 3rd 1968 Dr King, despite threats to his life, went to Memphis, Tennessee to support a strike by the city's garbage workers against low wages and intolerable working conditions.

33 Desmond Tutu was ordained in 1961 and lectured at a theological seminary. Later he went to London, where he obtained an M.A. from King's College. From 1972 to 1975 he served as an assistant director for the World Council of Churches.

South Africa. He was accused of being a traitor but became a popular world figure. P. W. Botha became President. Tutu was viewed as dangerous and his passport was cancelled. Protesters were beaten, arrested, imprisoned or even shot. In 1984, Tutu was awarded Noble Peace Prize. In the same year, Bishop Tutu visited Washington where he addressed the House Foreign Affairs subcommittee on Africa and fearlessly spoke out against the US President's South African policy:

> We are talking about a moral issue. ....racial segregation is evil, is immoral, is un-Christian, without remainder. In my view, the Reagan Administration's support and collaboration with it is equally immoral, evil and totally un-Christian. You are either for or against apartheid, and not by rhetoric. You are either in favour of evil, or you are in favour of good. You are either on the side of the oppressed or on the side of the oppressor. You can't be neutral.

Bishop Tutu became one of the most outstanding persons in the fight against apartheid which was politically conquered on 27th April 1994 under the leadership of Nelson Mandela. What is noted in the above references is that Christianity supplied him sufficient energy and inspiration required to fight that social evil called racism.

However, it is not possible for us to think of exclusive religious method limiting to Christianity but we need to refer to those models available to address the issue of racism meaningfully. For instance, George Yancey, Assistant Professor of Sociology, The University of North Texas, proposes two basic approaches that dominate how non-Christians attempt to handle racial problems. The first approach is what he calls the "color-blind" model. Whenever he teaches race/ ethnicity, he generally has students (who are usually white) that question why they even have to study about race and ethnicity. Their thinking is that if we can ignore race then racism will disappear. The focus of the color-blind model is that despite the past historical abuses that minorities have suffered, neither whites nor racial minorities today should enjoy any economic or social advantages because of their skin color. A second way non-Christians have attempted to deal with racism is through the "politically correct" model. The main argument of this model is that by empowering racial minorities we can overturn centuries of racial oppression. In this way the limitations of the color blind model, ignoring the historical and institutional racism that penetrates our society is corrected with deliberate efforts to institutionally reverse the effects of that racism. For example, racial minorities have historically been barred from employment opportunities. Because of this historical discrimination, it is contended that there should be overt attempts to increase economic opportunities for racial minorities.[34]

But both the models have its own weakness, for example, the color-blind model places too much confidence on the willingness of white Americans to seek justice in a meaningful way even if true racial reform inevitably leads to whites losing their historical, institutional advantages. The politically correct model is too eager to praise racial minorities and often fails to acknowledge the fact that sin knows no color.

Pope John Paul encouraged the Christian Church to give emphasis on education human of rights. At the Interreligious Assembly of 1999, Pope John Paul II declared: "The task before us ... is to promote a culture of dialogue. Individually and together, we must show that religious belief inspires peace, encourages solidarity, promotes justice and upholds liberty."[35] Racism is on the one hand an ideological and biological debate but the issue has been deepened when it is mixed with religion and religiously justifies the nature of devaluing human worth on the basis of colour and caste. In India, the crisis of the Dalits has been debated for long but they continue to face cultural, political and religious discrimination. In the case of the blacks in South Africa and America Christianity has contributed to a certain extent to restrict discrimination though much more freedom needs to be restored but in India it is still more difficult because Christianity though speaks of equality the definition of equality does not include caste equality and accommodates caste silently without ideological question. It is so because it contributes resources to the caste dominated Christian churches. For example, if

34 George Yancey, *Color Blindness, Political Correctness, or Racial Reconciliation: Christian Ethics and Race.*

35 Address at the Closing Ceremony, Vatican City [28 October 1999]: *L'Osservatore Romano* English edition [3 November 1999], 1-2.

caste is done away the practice of dowry will go away with it as per the legal abolition. Therefore, the (caste-based) Christian church, in her attempt to preserve the caste element systematically changed the word "dowry" to "gift" and collects huge sum of tithes after every marriage. They feel comfortable to demand and bargain the amount of gift which is seen only in India. However, the concern of the subject is that Christianity fails to address the issue of racism/casteism in India.

Conclusion

It is not easy for me to develop a model that would surpass the historical efforts of human history but we cannot also leave the issue without addressing it. The above discussion has made us clear about the length and wide of racism. It is not only biological, colour, political, religious and social but ideological definition made in order to create space by some sections of the people and therefore, to question its foundation and impact the responsibility has to be an integrated effort. The point 79 of Report of the World Conference against Racism, Racial Discrimination, Xenophobia and Related Intolerance, Durban, "We firmly believe that the obstacles to overcoming racial discrimination and achieving racial equality mainly lie in the lack of political will, weak legislation and lack of implementation strategies and concrete action by States, as well as the prevalence of racist attitudes and negative stereotyping;"[36]

(1) The whole national outlook needs to change in order to see the negativeness of racism and make policies according to the needs. There is a need to find alternative economic system that should have a proper distribution system to all citizens so that the weak are lifted up to fight any other forms of discrimination.

(2) There is a need to develop non-racial education system which would provide clear understanding of human rights and humanhood of every individual.

36 Report of the World Conference against Racism, Racial Discrimination, Xenophobia and Related Intolerance, Durban, 31 August - 8 September 2001.

(3) It is necessary for the Christians to understand religion from the perspective of the margins and interpret not simply to formulate idealist theory like tribal theology and Dalit theology but make it as a force that can question the social structure for the sake of manifesting human equality in a true sense.

5

"Look, they are one People"
A Theological Perspective on the Babel Narrative (Gen 11:1-9) for Ending Racism

Eyingbeni Hümtsoe-Nienu[1]

Introduction

Physical anthropology traces human origin to a single species.[2] It would be safe to say that "there was a time when humanity was just one race!" (cf., v. 6a). The plurality of human races emerged with time and there was no stopping the deluge of racial damages brought forth by incessant storm of social, political, biological, cultural or even religious imperialism. Racism as "Opinions and actions of the proponents of racial superiority or discrimination"[3] when juxtaposed with ideologies of racial supremacy, it weakens the fabric of human relationship and leaves threadbare the sense of mutual belongingness.

The reality of racial diversity today is generally met with two reactions: affirm or reject. The latter has resulted in ethnic cleansing while the former generates tolerance. But beyond these two reactions, a

---

1 Dr. Eyingbeni Hümtsoe-Nienu teaches Christian Doctrine and Gender Theologies at Clark Theological College, Mokokchung, Nagaland.

2 Roy Williams, *Keywords: A Vocabulary of Culture and Society* (London: Fontana Press, 1983), 249.

3 *Ibid*, 249.

third is called for – celebration – of colors. Blumenbach's classification (1787) of humanity into Caucasian, Mongolian, Malayan, Ethiopian and American Indian and marked by outer skin color white, yellow, brown, black and red[4] respectively may not necessarily be taken literally. However, the racial divide along the lines of color – among many other related factors like class, caste, nationality, gender, etc. – has blurred human's ancient idea of a common origin. To revive this thought would give human races the room to accommodate people of other races. This essay will emphasize on the importance of celebrating racial diversity, attributing it to divine origin, and attempt to show how God's plan of perpetuating racial diversity is actualized in the genomics of his begotten son, Jesus Christ. This Christological premise will direct a sketch of anti-racist approach, particularly with significance for Christian community.

The Sin of Babel: Opposing God's Heterogenous Mandate

There are apparently "gaps" in understanding the reason behind God's punitive judgment on the tower/city. "Pride" and "Fear" are two common renderings of the Shinarite's motive for building the structure. Strawn's dismissal of the first hint and alluding to the second one is significant. He advises reading the Babel narrative in its larger and also immediate literary context. "There," he says "we find that God created humans precisely to fill the earth and steward it.[5] Christian anthrogony (origin of humans) is primarily based on the idea of the *imago Dei* (Image of God; Gen 1: 27). The injunction that follows creation in God's image is for humanity to be "fruitful and multiply" (v. 28). Interestingly, the same idea is repeated after the Noahic Flood – God...said to them, "Be fruitful and multiply, and fill the earth" (9:1b, 7). Strawn declares, "In this larger perspective,

4 *Ibid*, 249. For a derivative understanding of "race" see Paul Gilroy, *After Empire: Melancholia or Convivial Culture* (Oxfordshire: Routledge, 2004), 31ff.

5 Brent A. Strawn, "Holes in the Tower of Babel," www.global.oup.com/obso/focus/focus_on_towerbabel/ (Accessed November 3, 2015). Jerome goes with "pride". Cf., *The New Jerome Biblical Commentary*, Eds., Raymond E. brown, Joseph A. Fitzmyer and Roland E. Murphy (Bangalore: TPI, 1995), 18.

the hunkering down is a refusal to fulfill the creational mandate."[6] He further explains that "God's punishment, while definitely a reversal of human desire, is not negative: it actually enables the humans to comply with God's initial command."[7] Hence, beyond the two factors, pride and fear, "rebellion" is obviously the immediate cause of their forced dispersion; because the people rebelled against God's command to be fruitful.

"Fruitfulness" can well be seen from the perspective of racial plurality that marks our world today. What strikes as fundamental to the command of God to be fruitful is the affirmative proclamation of God that creation indeed "was very good" (v. 31). The goodness of human diversity is to be traced back to the original intention of God. However, the role of sin turned God's good design to an upsetting one. Commenting on fruitfulness (1:28), Calvin marks that "God could himself indeed covered the earth with a multitude of men (sic); but it was his will that we should proceed from one fountain, in order that our desire of mutual concord might be greater, and that each might the more freely embrace the other as his flesh...Any inequality which is contrary to this arrangement is nothing else than corruption of nature which proceeds from sin."[8]

Our common humanity and divine mandate and approval for racial plurality, as a symbol of fruitfulness, are reasons why racism is sinful. It is a sin because first, we violate God and second we violate our fellow human being/s. The two levels of violation cannot be separated because God has made us with a common principle – his image. Calvin succinctly puts, "since they (human) bear the image of God engraven on them, He deems himself violated in their person... no one can be injurious to his (sic) brother without wounding God himself."[9] Any attempt to thwart racial plurality is a direct confrontation to the principle of divine life with which humanity is

6 Ibid. Cf., Walter Brueggermann, *Genesis: Interpretation* (Atlanta: John Knox, 1982); Terence Fretheim E, *God and World in the Old Testament: A Relational Theology of Creation* (Nashville, TN: Abingdon, 2005).

7 Ibid.

8 John Calvin, *Commentaries on the Book of Genesis*, Vol. I, Trans John King (Grand Rapids, MI: Baker Books, 2009 [500th Anniversary Edition]), 97-8.

9 Ibid., 295-96.

made and supposed to live by. Strawn rightly mentions that the story of Babel can -

> ...be seen as an early eye witness to the importance – indeed, the divine legitimation – of pluralism and diversity. There is, according to the story, a kind of unity (national, linguistic, otherwise) that God does not will and a diversity (national, linguistic, otherwise) that God does will.[10]

Raciological models have varied over the years. Extremisms in modern history have swung between dualism and assimilation.

(a) *Dualism* of the Nazis advocated the idea of "pure stock" and divided people into pure and impure stock. The evolutionary concept of race meant that only the superior race, i.e., the Aryans would have the natural right and potency to survive; being the fittest. The rest would have to be annihilated by natural rule because they are considered not fit for survival – human nonetheless.[11] This model is rife with supremacist attitude that goes to the extent of dismissing people of other race as "infrahuman"[12] because dualism purports that between duality whatever is superior is the noble one and thus naturally have the right to overthrow the lower form of life – all non-Aryans. This idea of race is not only gross but borders on insanity and should not find a place in modern society.

(b) *Assimilation* of the Sangh Parivar in India has, of late, come under severe criticism for advocating "sameness" or uniformity ideal. The boiling pot analogy best fits this idea. In this case, race is consolidated with the Hindu religion and culture, whereby adherents of the religion are by default considered as having acceptable racial affinity. The claim that everyone is originally a Hindu (*Ghar Wapasi* – Homecoming – is one such example) is one way of arguing for assimilation into one unified religious whole. One's particular racial identity, with all its cognate realities, are lost into a common

---

10 Strawn, "Holes in the tower of Babel." Cf. Theodore Hiebert, "The Tower of Babel and the Origin of the World's Cultures," *Journal of Biblical Literature* 126 (2007): 29-58.

11 This ideology is well depicted in the 95 minutes video documentary by Ben Stein, *Expelled: Intelligence not Allowed* (Premise Media Corporation, 2008).

12 Cf., Gilroy, *After Empire,* 31ff.

cauldron of unity and what potentially survives is the 'one' identity – Hinduness. This oneness is defined not so much by body as by religious affiliation. The concept of Hinduism as *sanadhana dharma* (original religion) takes precedence over other race-related elements. This agenda, which is also commonly called saffronization or brahmanization, goes beyond diet-politics.[13] It burrows deeper into the recess of democratic principles, including secularism, that recognize diversity in all race, religion and ethnicity and chews away at it gradually but surely. It is as equally divisive as the Nazi's agenda and perpetuating it in any form is also equally repulsive.

Highlighting the intensity of the evil of racism and its effects, Williams rightly states,

> Physical, cultural, and socio-economic differences are taken up, projected and generalized, and so confused that different kinds of variations are made to stand for or imply each other. The prejudice and cruelty that then often follow, or that are rationalized by the confusions, are not only evil in themselves; they have also profoundly complicated, and in certain areas placed under threat, the necessary language of the (non-prejudicial) recognition of human diversity and its actual communities.[14]

Christians or otherwise, the very fact of our common humanity warrants that people who looks "not-like-us" be looked at as "like-us." Without a shift in race perspective the goodness of racial diversity with celebratory attitude would not be possible. Moreover, the evil that accompanies racism – in all its corresponding consequences – will only breed more violence, hatred, and death among humans. Celebrating racial diversity is indispensable to a fruitful human co-existence. The Shinarites wanted homogeneity, God desired heterogeneity. In Jesus Christ, the plan of God to embrace diversity finds perfection.

---

13 Kunal Pradhan et. al., "Beef, Ban & Bloodshed," *India Today* (Oct 19, 2015), 26-33.

14 Williams, *Keywords,* 250.

Babel Redeemed: Christological Framework for Racial Unity

The idea of racial superiority, purity, originality and/or uniformity is untenable in a globalized multiracial context today. Any Babel agenda and confusion therein can be resolved in the person of the universal Christ who is the embodiment of racial concord. In him, the Jews, Canaanites, Greeks, Romans and other races and tribes find meaning not because he was God incarnate but because in him the fullness of God dwelt bodily (Col 2). His humanity expresses the reality of his racial identity that becomes the matrix of him being loved, revered, hated and even crucified. When Paul declares Jesus to be the last Adam (Rom 5: 12ff; 2Cor 15: 22, 45), he sets him over against the first Adam who is "a type of fallen humanity"[15] and contrasts with Jesus who exemplifies "humanity in its perfection."[16] In Jesus, then, we see not only a new kind of humanity but a perfect representative of what humanity - with all its racial connotations - should be. Three pillars to support racial unity in diversity are underlined.

(a) *Jesus' embodiment of racial diversity*: The assimilative agenda was squashed as was the building projects of the residents of Shinar. They had to be forcefully "scattered" by God "over the face of the earth" (Gen 11:8). They wanted to consolidate themselves on their own terms but God had other plans for them and through them. However, Jesus' incarnation ultimately fulfilled God's plan of embracing peoples, nations, tribes and tongues – all constitutive elements of race. His genealogy itself portrays his mixed ancestry beginning from Adam in Lk 3: 23-38 and Abraham in Mt 1: 1-16.

The racial composition of Jesus comprises of Canaanites, Moabites, Jews and nomadics (Mt 1). As Wright points out, "Jesus the Jew" had "Gentile blood!"[17] The mixture of races in the blood of the human Jesus is symbolical of God's purposeful reenactment of the Genesis mandate for humanity to be fruitful and replenish the earth. Jesus, the last Adam, recapitulates this divine instruction within his own humanness by physically embodying diverse racial identities.

15 Donald Guthrie, *New Testament Theology* (Leicester/Illinois: InterVarsity Press, 1981), 334.

16 *Ibid.*, 335.

17 Christopher J. H. Wright, *Knowing Jesus through the Old Testament* (Downers Grove, IL: InterVarsity Press, 1992), 5.

That both Luke and Matthew traces his lineage to ancestors of varying races indicate his rootedness in history, the locus of organic human process (Cf., Gal 3:16)[18] and also his universal significance as representing all peoples/races in himself.

(b) *Jesus' espousal of racial dignity*: Every race is worthy of God's intervention. They Shinarites were spread to the ends of the earth to fulfill the divine mandate of filling the earth – a symbolic injunction to proclaim the dignity of people from all corners representing diverse races. Xenophobia of the Shinarites is clearly manifest in their attempt to huddle up within their exclusive community and land. By Jesus' descent of several races (Matt 1), represented by the nomadic Abraham, the Israelite Jacob, the Canaanite Rahab, and the Moabite Ruth and also he had no sense of shame to declare his affinity to those patriarchs and matriarchs of diverse "stock" (Cf., Mk 6:3; Jn 2:12; Acts 1:14; 1Cor 9:5). By this he dignifies all races because in him people of different races share a part in his divine incarnation.

In his ministry as well the Samaritans, Romans, Canaanites, Jews and other gentiles received equal access to this God/man (Cf., Jn 4: 1-42; Lk 7:1-9; Mt 15: 21-28). The question of racial supremacy and fight for proving to be the fittest race are balanced out by his affirming the unity of all people with the words, "Great is your faith! Let it be done for you as you wish" (Mt 15:28). In this episode, Jesus not only commends the faith of a woman non-Jew (the Jews perceived themselves as the divinely privileged race and saw the Gentiles as "dogs") but affirms the dignity of Syrophoenicians, just as much as he did of the Hebrews (cf., v. 24-26). Jesus' universal mission began not by endorsing Jewish superiority and hierarchy but by advocating the dignity of all races. In embracing peoples of all ethnicity and races, he became "fruitful" and "filled the earth" (Cf., Mt 28: 18-20).

(c) *Jesus' execution of racial justice*: The Shinarites' zealous will to not "be scattered aboard upon the face of the whole earth" (Gen 11. 4b) as an attempt to inhibit the multi national creational purpose of God is acted upon when God declared, "Come let us go down and confuse their language there…so the Lord scattered them

18 Cf., John A. T. Robinson, *The Human Face of God* (London: SCM Press, 1977), 43-47.

abroad from there over the face of all the earth (vv 7-8)." This is what happened to Jonah when he attempted to hijack God's redemptive purpose to the people of Nineveh (Cf., Jon 4:2). When the people would not do it willingly, God had to ensure that no race was out of God's redemptive reach by stepping in and overturning human plans that contradicts God's will. God's dispersion of the descendants of Noah in Gen 11 ultimately had universal scope and in Jesus "God opened the way to the universalizing of his redemptive grace to all nations."[19]

Racial hegemony, under the veneer of cultural and religious sanctity today, never found favor with Jesus. He openly challenged such arrogance as contradicting divine kingdom values (Cf. Mk 10: 25, 17-27; Rev 7: 9-10). Matthew Henry rightly remarked that "grace does not run in the blood."[20] In Jesus, people of all races are "justified" to stand before God and to be acknowledged as his children. Apostle Paul's declaration that in Christ "there is no longer Jew or Greek….; for you are all one in Christ" (Gal 3:28) seals humanity's debate on racial hierarchy. His grace has won over divisive bloodlines and secured freedom for all from all racial oppression.

However, humanity is not hopeless. The universal Christ, by his bodily incarnation, his message and life, redeems people from destroying one another on xenophobic grounds. Jesus symbolically redeems Babel-

(a) By putting an end to hostility against God's will to create and sustain a world with diversity.
(b) By ushering in an inclusive imagery of race equality.
(c) By freely making all people God's children, born of one "seed" – Christ (Gal 3:16).
(d) By consolidating human families in and through him to build a kingdom of God.

19 Wright, *Knowing Jesus*, 44.

20 Matthew Henry, *Matthew Henry's Commentary: Matthew to John*, Vol. 6 (Peabody, MA: Hendrickson, 1991), 3.

Conclusion

In the incident following the racially motivated alleged murder of a tribal from Northeast India Nido Tania on January 29, 2014 in the capital city of India, social media sites were rife with comments that ranged from expression of anger to vindictive outbursts. The recent March 3, 2015 incident involving the lynching of the alleged Bangladeshi-Indian (Gal 3:28) was met with similar reactions. Racially motivated violence has been an ugly part of human history. More so, when race clashes with other ideologies linked to gender, class, caste, religion, ethnicity, nationality etc. Then the outcome is more often than not, disastrous.

In chronicling the life of the anti-apartheid champion and first black President of South Africa, Nelson Mandela, Rod Green notes how Mandela "regularly experienced the humiliation of having white students move to sit further away from him"[21] in lecture halls in the university of Witwatersrand (Wit in short). But because of the University's policy of non-discrimination, decreed in the first Principal's, Prof. Jan Hofmeyr's, words that Wit "should know no distinctions of class, wealth, race or creed," Wit was instrumental in railing against racism in South Africa[22] and influencing race activists like Mandela, among others. On the streets, Racism was so embedded in South Africa that made Mandela claim that, when he was on the run from police arrests, "to find it easier to effect a disguise if 'I did not walk as tall or stand as straight'."[23] But he fought hard against it and overcame it, becoming the first colored President of SA!

Racism is an unnecessary vice in modern history. It was not designed by God. God's good intention for racial diversity is exploited to forward one's race and related identities like tribe, ethnicity, language, nationality, etc. What was meant to be fruitful instruction is turned into destructive habits. Instead of wanting to comply with God's directive, human beings continue to rebel and find ways to perpetuate parochialism and trying to building a city with a tower

21 Rod Green, *Mandela - The Life Story of Nelson Mandela* (London: Constable and Robinson Ltd, 2013), 48.

22 *Ibid*, 48-9.

23 *Ibid*, 117.

for one's own race and people. This invites a veritable Babel in our societies and nations.

The covenantal sign between Noah and God (Gen 9:8-17), is a fitting correlative with the succeeding story of the Tower of Babel. The command to be "fruitful and multiply" (v. 7) is followed by the sign of the rainbow. The rainbows can well represent the diverse races on the face of the earth. What makes it significant is that each color is distinguishable and yet one color only makes the next one stand out. The harmony of different colors accentuates each other so that we see them as a unit – a people with many colors. When human beings come together in harmony God recognizes that there will certainly be "nothing that they propose to do will (now) be impossible for them" (Gen 11:6b). This can be cited to serve not racist purposes but to serve a common purpose wherein the favor of God, who is anything but racist, rests. For after all, humanity is God's creation and we have a common origin in God who acknowledges, "Look, they are one people!"

6

Race-(ism) A Threat to Social Harmony A Sociological Perspective

Temjensosang[1]

The concepts of race have long figured in accounts offered by social scientist of the social world. Although, once held to refer to objective differences between human populations entailing a view of races as discrete groups identifiable by some phenotypical feature and with distinct and unalterable characteristics, the term has come to have a much less stable meaning[1] or rather obsolete.

For purpose of our discourse, a human race is defined as a group of people with certain common inherited features that distinguish them from other groups of people. However, today, all men of whatever race they belong are currently classified by the anthropologist and biologist as belonging to the one species, Homo sapiens (Human being). This perspective gives more objective meaning when we see human in the context of larger environmental scenario. This is another way of saying that the differences between human races are not great, even though they may appear so, i.e. black vs white vs yellow vs red skin. All races of mankind in the world can interbreed (inter-marry) because they have so much in common. All races share 99.99+% of the same genetic materials which means that

1 Dr. Temjensosang is the Associate Professor and Head of the Department of Sociology at Nagaland University, Lumami, Nagaland.

division of race is largely subjective, and that the original 3-5 races were also probably just subjective descriptions as well.

Friends, all I know about human race are these few groups of humanity classified on their physical features and appearance but beyond which I have no scientific proofs which makes them different. These are the Black skin Negro, the Red skin or Indian Race, the white or Caucasian race occupies all of Europe, the Yellow or Mongolian and the Samoids, Esquimaux, and Tartars.[2] I have also no contention even if there were more than a dozen of skin colours should these humanity co-exist peacefully and harmoniously.

My attention is drawn and indeed every body's attention is drawn when we suffix three letters "ISM" into the concept of race it turns into racism which gives a negative connotation. "ism" as far as I can define is divisive, Hippocratic, jealous, complexion, hatred, prejudice, discrimination, superior-inferior feeling, beautiful-ugly feeling, rich-poor feeling, master-servant, etc. etc. and at the larger social structure it generates social stratification. Racism indeed is a tool in the hands of the dominant groups.

The concepts of race and racism are of relatively recent origin. Although, ideas about human differences on the basis of colour and phenotypic characteristics already occurred in earlier societies, however the present meaning of the concept of "race" only became current toward the end of the eighteenth century subsequent to the French and American revolutions. The notion of "race" thus originated in modern times and has changed with the evolution of modern society. As Hannaford (1996) shows, the introduction of this concept constituted the culmination of a complex development in modern thought regarding descent, heredity and human differences. After the Reformation movement popularly enlightenment period in Europe the explanations of the origin of people in terms of religion or reason was increasingly displaced by a racial discourse in which anatomy, bloodlines, climate, geographical location and language[3] were central point of study.

The distinctions between negative evaluations of phenotypic differences in skin colour, in hair colour, in the colour and shape of eyes, in the shape of the skull and so on has for a long time been a central element of the ideology of racism. These kinds of differences were used as explanations for differences in culture and in mental properties. By the late 19th century and early 20th century this mode of thinking was common in the Western world. It was developed in academia and spread throughout society (Shipman, 1994). It was used to justify practices such as slavery and colonialism. Therefore, "Race" was construed as a social fact and thus has an object of scientific inquiry.[4]

By the late 19th century and early 20th century the concept of "race" acquired major political significance too. "Race" as a dominant and widely accepted ideological concept in Western thought was no longer only used to explain socio-cultural differences but, in particular, also to justify inequalities at the political level. The shift to a political implementation of racist doctrines at the national level was made in the 1930s by the National Socialists, under the leadership of Hitler in Germany. This development culminated in genocide during the Second World War, when the Nazis killed six million Jews and at least two hundred thousand Gypsies in gas chambers.[5]

After the Second World War, at the request of the United Nations Educational Scientific and Cultural Organization (UNESCO), authorities in the social sciences examined the concept of race. Thereby in their declaration of 1950, they argued that "race" is less a biological phenomenon than a social myth, for all practical social purposes 'race' is not so much a biological phenomenon as a social myth. The myth of 'race' has created an enormous amount of human and social damage. In recent years it has taken a heavy toll in human lives and caused untold suffering. It still prevents the normal development of millions of human beings and deprives civilization of the effective co-operation of productive minds. The biological differences between ethnic groups should be disregarded from the standpoint of social acceptance and social action.[6]

"Race" is therefore a social construction invented by people. It is first and foremost a discursive category, "the organizing category of those ways of speaking, systems of representation and social practices (discourses) which utilize a loose, often unspecified set of differences in physical characteristics such as skin colour, hair texture, physical and bodily features, and so forth--as *symbolic markers* in order to differentiate one group socially from another." The UNESCO therefore advocated dropping the term "race" and replacing it by a more neutral term called "ethnic group." Hence, "Race" no longer existed; that is to say, biological science has abandoned the very concept. Racism, however, did continue to exist in the social world manifested in different terms as ethnic groups, cultural groups, etc. etc. and are studied under multiculturalism.

Friends, if the term race ceased to use from the biological science as discussed above then, today, I strongly claim that racism is definitely a social-cultural product which is structurally generated by society itself for accomplishment of certain social and individual ends. As a social scientist by training and sociologist by profession I wish to substantiate my argument based on available Sociological theories.

Sociology has three main perspectives while looking at social phenomena and these perspectives gives us the theoretical orientation which I proposed for consideration and deliberations; here are:

1. Functionalist Theory argues that for race and ethnic relations to be functional and thus contribute to the harmonious conduct and stability of society, racial and ethnic minorities must assimilate into that society. Assimilation is a process by which a minority becomes socially, economically, and culturally absorbed within the dominant society. The assimilation perspective assumes that to become fully fledged members of society, minority groups must adopt as much of the dominant society's culture as possible, particularly its language, mannerisms, and goals for success, and thus give up much of its own culture. Assimilation-ism stands in contrast to racial cultural pluralism the maintenance and persistence of one's culture, language, mannerisms, practices, art, and so on.

Many nations today have the notion of mono-culture instead of multiculturalism, such as Americanization, Canadianizatio, Indianization, Koreanization, etc., the spirit of multiculturalism (peaceful coexistence of multiple culture) is often pushed aside by the dominant culture, hence resulted in ethnic violence, racial hatred, etc.

2. Symbolic Interaction Theory addresses two issues: first, the role of social interaction in reducing racial and ethnic hostility, and second, how race and ethnicity is socially constructed. Symbolic interaction-ism asks, what happens when two people of different racial or ethnic origins come into contact with each other, and how can such interracial or inter-ethnic contact reduce hostility and conflict? Contact theory, which originated with the psychologist Gordon Allport argues that the contact must be between individuals of equal status; the parties must interact on equal ground. The contacts between equals must be sustained; short-term contact will not decrease prejudice. The participants must agree upon social norms favouring equality.

3. Conflict Theory assumes the premise that class-based conflict is an inherent and fundamental part of social interaction. To the extent that racial and ethnic conflict is tied to class conflict, conflict theorists argue that class inequality must be reduced to lessen racial and ethnic conflict in society. The current "class versus race" controversy concerns the question of whether class or race is more important in explaining inequality and its consequences or whether they are of equal importance. Those focusing primarily upon class conflict, have argued that class and changes in the economic structure are sometimes more important than race in shaping the life chances of different groups. Sociologists focusing primarily on the role of race argue the opposite: They say that race has been and is relatively more important than class though class is still important in explaining and accounting for inequality and conflict in society and that directly addressing the question of race forthrightly is the only way to solve the country's race problems.

A recent variety of the conflict perspective propounded by Andersen and Collins is the inter-section perspective. This perspective refers to the interactive or combined effects of racism, classism (elitism), and gender in the oppression of people. Inter-sectional theory posits that any person is socially located in a position that involves race, class, and gender and, thus, looking at only one of them to explain their status is incomplete. This perspective notes that not only are the effects of gender and race intertwined, but also both are intertwined with the effects of class. Class, along with race and gender, are integral components of social structure, according to the inter-section perspective.

Conflict theory originated from the works of Karl Marx whose basic premises centred on the notion of 'mode of production.' In this he identified in every stage of human societies there are two classes of people, i.e., the 'Bourgeoisie and Proletariat' he also called to this as "Haves and Have Not." In every succeeding stage of society the nature of conflict may be different but the premises of conflict remain the same that is economy.[7]

Having cleared my stand on the broad theoretical framework as stated above I wish to narrow down the problem and contextualize the issue of racism in India. The framer of the constitution of India has steadfastly worked to make India a secular state therefore in a bird's eye view the sovereignty of the country survives through secularism. However, a worm's eye view reveals the fact that India has a massive racial and ethnic unrest and this are manifested in different ugly situation such as hate speech, communal row, gender harassment, the ethnic uprising, remarks against narrow eye, remarks against dark skin, tall or short physic, etc. A social lens carefully focused on the demographic composition of this largest democracy will find that India is composed of many race such as, Dravidian, Aryans, Indo-Aryan, Mongoloid, etc....a religion-cultural lens would see the dominant Hinduism suppressing the minority Muslim, Christian, Buddhist, Jain, Parses, Sikhs, etc. The configuration of the so-called "BHARAT," "INDIA" is a 'salad Powel' that has full of racial unrest. Since the recent past this country is witnessing the rising intolerance, some of the instances are; the racial attacked on the African students in Delhi 2014. Attacks on the northeastern whether in Delhi, Bangalore, Gurgaon, etc., the reasons for attacked being, the victims doesn't look like them, because they don't speak like them, they don't eat like them, dress like them therefore north easterner feels Delhi is not a safe haven for them or for that matters many cities in India.

Let us turn the table and see what happens if we are at the dominant group, in 2012 north easterners fled Bangalore, reason being they would be attacked by the Muslims a retaliation of what happened in Assam. In 2007, thousands of Hindi-speaking labourers fled from Assam after a series of massacres and bomb attacks. In May 2007, nine of them were killed and another 20 injured in violent attacks. In August 2007, 26 people from other parts of India were killed in a series of attacks over a period of six days. The members of Purbottar Hindustani Sanmelan (PHS) staged a hunger strike in Dispur to protest against the "merciless killings of innocent and defenceless Hindi-speaking people." Overall, 98 non-locals were killed in Assam during 2007. In March–April 2008, a banned Meitei outfit killed 16 non-locals in Manipur. PHS alleged that anti-social elements in Assam were carrying out a continuous hate campaign against the Hindi speakers in the region. In May 2009, nine Hindi speakers were killed in Assam and Manipur, after the attackers set around 70 houses ablaze. During 8–10 November 2010, 21 Hindi, Bengali and Nepali speakers were killed by a faction of the National Democratic Front of Bodoland (NDFB) in Assam. In January 2014, five men from Bihar were killed and another three were injured after being pulled out from a bus and shot at. In Meghalaya the non-indigenous people who are collectively called *Dkhars* are always the target of both the militant groups and other advocacy groups. All India statistics shows that Biharis are the worst victims of racial attacks.

My queries and inquisitiveness as to why one become a racist still continues. My work on 'self governing institutions of Nagas' was aimed at understanding how institutions have been the source of social control among the Naga society; in the process I also found out that establishing a village is an important aspect in the study of institutions. The fact is in many of the institutions and especially in the formation of village council only the first settlers have the privilege of occupying the first rank or the cabinets while the late comers are given the post of assistants. There is always in the air that all are equal but some are more than equal, therefore allocation of the post of assistants is a constant reminder of not being equal. Therefore, Naga society is governed not on the basis of capability, best person, and the ablest.[8] But Nagas are not an exceptional case rather it is universal everywhere. The point that disturbs me is the message "some are more than equal," in a democracy all are equal, but when some enjoys more than the equal it results in prejudice, discrimination, hatred, etc., this is the roots of racism.

Let me take an analogy from a psychological and cultural stand point. Take a piece of cloth such as a handkerchief. What is the function of a handkerchief? To wipe off sweat, clean our hands, wipe our mouth, and blow our nose and all menial tasks. Is the meaning of these functions in the cloth? No. It is in culture, in our human society which has taught us to view and regard a handkerchief in this way. You can take the same piece of cloth and make it into a shirt or a blouse and give it the functions of both protecting and celebrating our bodies. You can also take this same piece of cloth, add some red, some blue and some stars and turn it into a flag, and it becomes the signature of a people, symbolizing their group identity and nationality. And many are willing to die and kill for it, and others to stand at attention with tears in their eyes in a moment of triumph, like the many athletes at the Olympic Games as their national flag is raised in celebrated honour of their world-record victories. Consider Karch Kiraly, Captain of the United States Olympic volleyball team, which won the gold medal in both the 1984 and 1988 games, and who was been designated "The World's Best Volleyball Player" by the International Volleyball Federation. After the team won the gold medal at the 1984 games in Los Angeles, Kiraly declared: "I don't remember much about the last match for the gold in Los Angeles, and I don't remember the medal being put around my neck, but I'll never forget singing screaming the anthem as our flag went up just a little higher than the others." Over what? Over a mere piece of coloured cloth! Not just any cloth, however, but a cloth imbued with meaning, significance and national symbolism and in which we invest emotions that bring spin-tingling sensations in moments of victory or patriotism, or outrage when dishonoured, such as the 1989 political flap over the burning of the American flag.[9] The activity of a person is oriented to a given particular culture into which one is born; it is filled with emotions. Therefore, one sees its culture the most satisfying and best and everyone sees others from the perspective of one's own culture. Culture is relative therefore all culture looks similar, but the fact is every culture draw its own boundary eg; everybody said sati system, dowry system, child marriage are bad practices but why was it not stop by itself? If racism is bad practice why was it not stop by itself? There may have much explanation but the bottom line is society and culture still encourage. It is bad for the victim but honour and patriotism for the doer. Eg- Kulkarini was painted black by pouring colours on him by the shiv sainik in Mumbai for taking the initiative to launch a book "neither Dove nor Hawk" by a Pakistani author. Here, the paint attacked was contempt by many, but the attackers were honoured by their political party.

In all these argument I am only trying to say that racism is socially and structurally generated tool in the hands of dominant group that is inherent in human culture. Today the greatest threat to all humanity is global terrorism and it is the product of racism. Believe me racism was always present in all human societies, in ancient times there were free man and slaves, the Greeks had patrician and plebian, the feudal society had lords and serfs, today we have oppressors and oppressed.

I have attempted to bring to light various theories and contextualized to our situation but I have no solution at hand to solve this menace. The only ray of hope I see is, if Gandhi talks of non-violence and religious tolerance some less than hundred years ago let us appreciate that, but if Jesus have practice it more than two thousand years ago and commanded us to do the same let us follow him; because for Jesus there is no distinction between Jews and Greek for the same our Lord is Lord of all, abounding in richness for all who called on him; for who will call on the name of the Lord will be saved (Roman 10: 12-13), and yet again there is neither Jew nor Greek, there is neither slaves nor free man, there is neither male or female, for you are all one in Christ Jesus (Galatian 3:28) Only Jesus can heal the world.

References

1. *International Encyclopaedia of Social Sciences.*
2. http: chestofbooks.com/reference. Platt. I, A Library Of Wonders And Curiosities Found In Nature And Art, Science And Literature.
3. Racism: wikipedia, free encyclopedia.
4. Hannaford, Ivan. 1996. *Race, The History of an Idea in the West.* Washington DC: Woodrow Wilson Center Press/ London: Johns Hopkins University Press.
5. Montagu, Ashley. 1963. *Race, Science and Humanity.* New York: Van Nostrand Reinhold Company.
6. Temjensosang, 2013. *Self Governing Institutions of Nagas.* Akansha Publishing House, New Delhi.

7. Goldhagen, Daniel. 1996. *Hitler's Willing Executioners: Ordinary Germans and the Holocaust.* London: Little, Brown and Company.
8. Temjensosang (et al), 2015. *Historicity, Cultural Diversity and Identities in North East India.* Heritage Publication, Dimapur: Nagaland.
9. Gupta, R. L. 1991, *Political Theory.* Sultan Chand and Sons, New Delhi pp. 375-398.

7

Law and Racism
Indian Legal Perspective

P. B. M. Basaiawmoit[1]

Thank you for the honour to make a presentation at this august national seminar on a very contemporary issue faced by many in this vast countryand drawing eminent personalities for peace and justice being held at Clark Theological College, Aolijen, Mokokchung, Nagaland but am surprised that you have asked me to make a brief introduction into the Indian legal perspective on racism though am not trained in any legal discipline. Thank you too for the limitation of time since am not keeping in good health and would not be able to make reflections on each of the provisions incorporated here for our knowledge and study but am sure, all of us can feel the spirit and objectives of the constitutional provisions.

Racism

Allow me to at least give one quote on racism. "It may be defined as the hatred of one person by another - or the belief that another person is less than human because of skin, colour, language, custom, place of birth or factor that supposedly reveals the basic nature of that person. It has influenced wars, slavery, the formation of nations and legal codes."[1]

1 Rev. Dr. Prechard B. M. Basaiawmoit is a member of the Peace and Justice Committee, Presbyterian Churches of India, Shillong, Meghalaya.

Constitutional Provisions against Racism[2]

The Constitution of India is a complex document, adopted on 26 November, 1949 and came into force on 26 January, 1950. Let us see some of the provisions there-in.

1. The Preamble assures Justice in terms of social, economic and political; Liberty of thought, belief, faith and worship; Equality of status and opportunity, and to promote them all; Fraternity, i.e. assuring the dignity of the individual as well, the unity and integrity of the nation. It may be added that "pluralism is the keystone of Indian culture and religious tolerance is the bedrock of Indian secularism."
2. The most important components of Indian secularism are:
   a) Right to Equality (Arts 13 - 18);
   b) Right to Freedom (Arts. 19 – 22);
   c) Right against Exploitation (Arts. 23 and 24);
   d) Right of Freedom of Religion (Arts. 25 – 28);
   e) Right to Cultural and Educational Rights (Arts. 29 and 30);
   f) Right to constitutional remedies (Arts. 32).

On the Right to Equality, Art. 15 prohibits against any citizen on grounds of religion, race, caste, sex or place of birth or any of them. And in 2005, this Article was further amended for providing reservations in admission for Scheduled Caste and Scheduled Tribe and Backward Classes in private unaided educational institutions.

With regard to employment, Art. 16 (1) and (2) explicitly states thus:

(1) There shall be equality of opportunity for all citizens in matters relating to employment or appointment to any office under the State.

(2) No citizen shall, on grounds only of religion, race. caste, sex, descent, place of birth, residence or any of them, be ineligible for, or discriminated against in respect of, any employment or office under the State."

Other Special Provisions for Scheduled Tribes in the Constitution

Article 330 is a provision for special provisions in the House of the People (Lok Sabha) for Scheduled Castes and Scheduled Tribes while Art. 332 is for providing reservation of seats for Scheduled Castes and Scheduled Tribes in State Legislative Assemblies.

Article 335 pertains to claims of members of the Scheduled Castes and Scheduled Tribes to services and posts: "The claims of the members of the Scheduled Castes and the Scheduled Tribes shall be taken into consideration, consistently with the maintenance of efficiency of administration, in the making of appointments to services and posts in connection with the affairs of the Union or of a State." Further, the Constitution (Eighty-second Amendment) Act, 2000, sec 2 was inserted to this Article and took effect from 08/09/2000 whereby it states: "Provided that nothing in this article shall prevent in making of any provision in favour of the members of the Scheduled Castes and the Scheduled Tribes for relaxation in qualifying marks in any examination or lowering the standards of evaluation, for reservation in matters of promotion to any class or classes of services or posts in connection with the affairs of the Union or of a State."

Article 338 A inserted by the Constitution (Eighty-ninth Amendment) Act, 2003, sec. 3 and became operative since 19/02/2004, pertains to setting up of National Commission for Scheduled Tribes which duties include:

"(a) to investigate and monitor all matters relating to the safeguards provided for the Scheduled Tribes under this Constitution or under any other law for the time being in force or under any order of the Government and to evaluate the working of such safeguards;

(b) to inquire into specific complaints with respect to the deprivation of rights and safeguards of the Scheduled Tribes;

(c) to participate and advise on the planning process of socio-economic development of the Scheduled Tribes and to evaluate the progress of their development under the Union and any State;..."

Regional Language(s) for Communication

Articles 345, 346 and 347 make provisos for language or languages to be adopted by a State Legislature for official purposes within a State and also any other language spoken by a substantial proportion of a State to be officially recognised.

Article 350A pertains to facilities for instruction in mother-tongue at primary stage while Article. 350B pertains to appointment by the President of India a Special Officer for linguistic minorities whose duty is "to investigate all matters relating to the safeguards provided for linguistic minorities under this Constitution and report to the President..."

Scheduled Areas and Tribal Areas

Article 244 is exclusively for administration of Scheduled and Tribal Areas and accordingly, the Fifth Schedule to the Constitution was added and which shall apply to the administration and control of the Scheduled Areas and Scheduled Tribes in any State except in the States of Assam, Meghalaya, Tripura and Mizoram and the Sixth Schedule to the Constitution was introduced for administration of tribal areas in Assam, Meghalaya, Tripura and Mizoram. In addition, there is Article 244A making proviso for formation of an autonomous State comprising certain tribal areas in Assam and creation of local Legislature or Council of Ministers or both therefore.

Article 371:

"Article 371A. Special Provision with respect to the State of Nagaland ____

(1) Notwithstanding anything in this Constitution, ___

(a) no Act of Parliament in respect of __
  (i) religious or social practices of the Nagas,
  (ii) Naga customary law and procedure,
  (iii) administration of civil and criminal justice involving decisions according to Naga customary law,
  (iv) ownership and transfer of land and its resources,
  apply to the State of Nagaland unless the Legislative Assembly of Nagaland by a resolution so decides."

"Article 371G. Special Provision with respect to the State of Mizoram

Notwithstanding in this Constitution,

(a) no Act of Parliament in respect of

(i) religious or social practices of the Mizos,

(ii) Mizo customary law and procedure,

(iii) administration of civil and criminal justice involving decisions according to Mizo customary law,

(iv) ownership and transfer of land,

shall apply to the State of Mizoram unless the Legislative Assembly of the State of Mizoram by a resolution so decides..."

Section 153-A, of the Indian Penal Code: Promoting enmity between different groups on grounds of religion, race, place of birth, residence, language, etc., and doing acts prejudicial to maintenance of harmony.____(1) Whoever ___

(a) by words, either spoken or written, or by signs or by visible representations or otherwise, promotes or attempts to promote, on grounds of religion, race, place of birth, residence, language, caste or community or any other ground whatsoever, disharmony or feelings of enmity, hatred or ill will between different religions, racial, language or regional groups or castes or communities, or

(b) commits any act which is prejudiced to the maintenance of harmony between different religious, racial, language or regional groups or castes or communities, and which disturbs or is likely to disturb the public tranquillity, or

(c) organizes any exercise, movement, drill or other similar activity intending that the participants in such activity shall use or be trained to use criminal force or violence or knowing it to be likely that the participants in such activity will use or be trained to use criminal force or violence, or participates in such activity intending to use or be trained to use criminal force or violence or knowing it to be likely that the participants in such activity will use or be trained to use criminal force or violence, against any religious,

> racial, language or regional group or caste or community and such activity, for any reason whatsoever causes or is likely to cause or alarm or a feeling of insecurity amongst members of such religious, racial, language or regional group or caste or community, shall be punished with imprisonment which may extend to three years, or with fine, or with both."[3]

Further in The Code of Criminal Procedure, 1973 as amended by The Code of Criminal Procedure (Amendment) Act, 2010, Section 505 states that in the case of making false statement, rumour, etc., with intent to create enmity, hatred or ill-will between different classes (implies ethnicity, race, colour, language and related matters), it is cognizable offence, non - bailable with imprisonment for 3 years or fine or both and that it can be dealt by any magistrate.[4]

There is also **Scheduled Castes and Scheduled Tribes (Prevention of Atrocities) Act, 1989 along with Rules, 1995**

International Laws, Charters and Conventions against Racism

Allow me to assure that the issue of racism has been thoroughly dealt with at the international level for a very long time and one might remember that economic sanctions was enforced on South Africa way back in the 1980s for its policy of apartheid which is racist in nature and theology. Even the issue of caste discrimination in India is looked upon as racist but no punitive action has been taken by the global family.

The Universal Declaration of Human Rights, an historic charter on human rights adopted on 10 December, 1948, has affirmed in its Preamble that "recognition of the inherent dignity of the equal inalienable rights, of all members of the human family, is the foundation of freedom, justice and peace in the world" and Article 2 states that "everyone is entitled to all rights set forth in this Declaration, without distinction of any kind, such as race, colour, sex, language, religion, political or other opinion, national or social origin, property, birth or other status."

In the Preamble to the **International Covenant on Economic, Social and Cultural Rights (ICESCR),** it is stated that "the ideal of free human beings enjoying freedom from fear and want can only be achieved if conditions are created whereby everyone may enjoy his economic, social and cultural rights, as well as his civil and political rights."

In Part II, Article 2 of the **International Covenant on Civil and Political Rights (ICCPR),** it states: "Each State Party to the present covenant undertakes to respect and to ensure to all individuals within its territory and subject to its jurisdiction the rights recognized in the present Covenant, without distinction of any kind, such as race, colour, sex, language, religion, political or other opinion, national or social origin, property, birth or other status."

Our Response

We know that persons from the Northeast have been targets of racial abuse, discrimination in different parts of India, but mainly at the National Capital Region and Karnataka and just recently, a Khasi youth returned home from studies in Karnataka due to over- zealous ragging. It was traumatic. He has since changed his line of studies but no more going out from home sweet home.

The constitutional provisos are perfect including those in IPC but who will bell the cat? or do we begin making people outside the region become aware of the ground reality? When we were students in Maharashtra, we faced a totally different reception - warm and hospitable. Now it is just the opposite and in unexpected places. It may be much deeper than racism and racialism. According to UN Convention on the Elimination of All Forms of Racial Discrimination, the term "racial discrimination" is defined as "any distinction, exclusion, restriction, or preference based on race, colour, descent or national or ethnic origin that has the purpose or effect of nullifying or impairing the recognition, enjoyment or exercise, on an equal footing, of human rights and fundamental freedoms in the political, economic, social, cultural or any other field of public life."[5]

Now we are faced with the issue of heterogeneity being converted into homogeneity through institutional racism also known as structural racism, state racism or systemic racism which is none other than "racial discrimination by governments, corporations, religions or educational institutions or other large organizations with the power to influence the lives of many individuals."[6]

Isn't the Hindutva agenda leading to this?

"The ideologues of Hindu nationalism defined the Hindu nation on the basis of a common culture, history and language... the Hindu nationalist ideologues wanted to define nationalism on the basis of exclusion of what they termed as followers of "foreign" religion and culture. ... Golwalkar calls upon non-Hindus to adopt Hindu culture and cease to be "foreigners", think of nothing else but the glory of the Hindu nation, else, be treated as non-citizens and claim no rights. "Minorities must accept the culture of the majority ----- which, according to them, is homogenous and monolithic, shorn of all its diversity."[7] We can discuss further on this much alive issue.

References

1. @2001 Action Defamation League, www.addl.org/hate-patrol/racism.asp quoted in Institutional Racism vis-a-vis Singularity of India, a presentation at the National Seminar on Singularity of India: Integration, Homogenization and Racism held at Imphal, Manipur, 28 – 29 January, 2013 and now included in the book, ' Is It Really Over ?', written by Prechard B. M. Basaiawmoit, pp. 122-127.
2. See P.M. Bakshi, The Constitution of India, Universal Law Publishing Co., New Delhi. All the extracts of Constitutional provisions are taken from this book.
3. B. M. Gandhi, Indian Penal Code, Second Edition, Eastern Book Company, Lucknow, pp. 224-5.
4. The Code of Criminal Procedure, 1973 (2 of 1974) as amended by the Code of Criminal Procedure (Amendment) Act, 2010 (41 of 2010) (w.e.f. 2-11-2010) with State Amendments, Universal Law Publishing Co., Pvt. Ltd., New Delhi, p. 329.
5. http://en.wikipedia.org/wiki/Racism, 17-12-2-12, quoted in Is It Really Over? p. 125.
6. ibid.
7. Irfan Engineer, Continuity and Change within the Sangh Parivar in Mainstream, Vol. LIII, No. 43, New Delhi, October 17, 2015, pp. 6 & 7.

8

Racism in Christian History

Toshi Aier[1]

Introduction

Racism pervades our world today. Racial notions, prejudices and fears are deeply rooted in the hearts and minds of human beings and continue to trouble relations between persons, human groups and nations. While, in order to assess the full weight of these phenomena, a detailed study of the roots and practice of racism in Christian history is called for, this paper will make no attempt to trace a complete history of racism or of Christian involvement in this regard due to paucity of time and sources. Rather, some highlights of this history will be indicated.

Colonialism and Racism

The history of racism in modern times begins with the African slave trade of the 16th and 17th centuries and the systematic extermination of the aboriginal people of the New World which accompanied it. At one period or another almost every nation in Europe profited from the traffic in African slaves and in North America chattel slavery became a basic institution of a powerful Protestant Christian society.

---

1 Mr. Toshi Aier teaches History of Christianity at the Clark Theological College, Mokokchung, Nagaland.

Colonisation by European powers was seen as a God-given opportunity for spreading the gospel to the heathen. It was a Christian duty, even when it led to the death of millions. Both Roman Catholic and Protestant churches encouraged colonisation. Typically, in Africa, missionaries would advance into new territories. Sooner or later they would sow discord, encouraging rebellion against unsympathetic local rulers. When bloodshed followed, the churches would appeal to European governments to intervene, and another territory would be annexed. This process seems to have accounted for more than half of European colonies in Africa. The belief of European Christians that other races were inferior led to colonisation and large scale abuse. The extirpating native peoples were only pagans and might even possess souls. They were slaves by nature. God had made them like that. Christian scholars and pseudo-scientists concurred.

The belief in the inherent superiority of the White race was promoted in the colonial era. Koranteng-Pipim describes it in this way:

> It is this spirit of inherent superiority that characterized the attitude of the European nations as they expanded overseas, competing for colonial power and the conversion of "heathen" natives. Since, the European conquerors possessed superior economic and military technology over the enslaved people of colour, they were able to explain the superiority of their cultural apparatus in terms of a superior human endowment.[2]

Another writer, Julian Go agrees:

> It would seem indisputable that modern colonialism in the early twentieth century involved racism. Indeed, during colonial occupation, colonizing groups were granted political, economic, and social privileges denied to the colonized, and the hierarchy was typically sustained by claims that the latter were racially inferior.[3]

2 S. Koranteng Pipim, 'Saved by Grace and living by Race; the Religion called Racism', in *The Journal of Adventist Theological Society*, 5 (2) 1994, 40.

3 Julian Go, 'Racism and Colonialism: Meanings and Difference and Ruling Practices in America's Pacific Empire,' *Qualitative Sociology*, 27 (1), 2004. 40.

These arguments about racism as a built-in and natural product of colonialism have been supported by scholarship in the social sciences. In *The Location of Culture*, Homi Bhabha remarks that the very purpose of colonial discourse was "to construe the colonized as a population of degenerate types on the basis of racial origin; in order to justify conquest."[4]

Following the suppression of the Atlantic slave trade in the 19th century the nations of Europe divided up Africa among themselves and by subterfuge and by military conquest colonized the people and proceeded to exploit their land and labour to benefit the metropolitan centres of Europe. The people of India, Indonesia and South-Eastern Asia were similarly dominated and exploited for European and American markets. In order to justify this massive expropriation of the wealth of black, brown and yellow people, the myth of the superiority of the white race was used, sometimes explicitly by way of biblical misinterpretation,[5] sometimes as a tacit presupposition. According to this myth the darker races of the world were held to be sub-human or innately inferior to all white people. They were divinely ordained to be "hewers of wood and drawers of water" for the Christian nations of Europe and America.[6]

White coloured skin, therefore, became the accepted standard of human beauty and all people were judged to be worthy of respect, civil rights and dignity in accordance with the affinity of their complexion to that standard. Even the oppressed peoples themselves accepted this standard and stratified their communities along colour lines.

The consequences of this development, which climaxed in Europe and America in the 19th century continues to affect the whole world. Carney is very straightforward in his critique of both colonial powers and missionaries for racializing Hutu and Tutsi categories

---

4 H. K. Bhabha, *The Location of Culture* (London: Routledge, 1994), 70.

5 One classic misinterpretation of the bible is the curse made by Noah on his son Ham-condemned, in his grandson Canaan to be his brother's slave (Ref Gen 9:24-27). Ham or Canaan as ancestors of the African peoples whom the whites had subjugated and consequently, they considered them marked with an indelible inferiority which destined them to serve whites forever.

6 Julian Go, 35-36.

in Rwanda, thus hardening previously fluid lines and introducing a tribal discourse that reaped a terrible harvest in the postcolonial period:

> Europeans created Hutu-Tutsi tensions if not the categories themselves. The ideological roots of Rwanda's postcolonial ethnic bloodletting stemmed not from primordial ethnic hatreds but from colonial manipulations between 1900 and 1960. Second, the key factor in this colonial manipulation was the catholic missionaries' racializing of the Hutu-Tutsi distinction. In turning flexible social categories into immutable racial identities, Rwanda's catholic leaders ensured the long-term division of Banyarwanda society along a Hutu-Tutsi tribal axis. Missionaries, colonial officials, and Rwandan elites all became locked in a dualistic political imagination of "Hutu" and "Tutsi."[7]

Nothwehr builds on those thoughts:

> Significantly, colonizers needed to justify their overtaking the property and persons of those they conquered. Justification required demonizing tribal peoples, exaggerating any conflicts among them. . . colonizers' most egregious practices were to arm one tribe, set that group up against their neighbours, and then employ them to "catch" their "enemy" and sell them to the slave traders. Their eliminating one group or favouring another over against the "others" was a genocidal activity. [8]

With their "divide and conquer" strategy to gain and maintain power, colonial powers, and missionaries to some extent, have thus spread the seed of ethnic and tribal hatred that continue to this day. Hallinan states that "divide and conquer was 19th and early 20th century colonialism's single most successful tactic of domination. It was also a disaster, one which still echoes in civil wars and regional

7 J. J. Carney, 'Beyond Tribalism: The Hutu-Tutsi Question and catholic Rhetoric in Postcolonial Rwanda,' *Journal of Religion in Africa*, 42, 2012, 173.

8 D. M. Nothwehr, *That they May be One: Catholic Social Teaching on Racism, Tribalism and Xenophobia* (Maryknoll, N.Y: Orbis Books, 2008), 5.

tensions across the globe."[9] With their military and economic controls, colonial powers not only broke colonized groups into smaller tribes and ethnic groups, they also worked to keep these smaller entities from uniting against them. They intentionally set small tribes or groups against each other in order to easily control them, their lands and territories.[10]

White racism and its consequences are ubiquitous. But its deepest and most harmful penetration is in Western Europe, the United States and Southern Africa. Almost every aspect of civilization-science, religion, law, economics, politics, etiquette and art, have been infected with white racism. All the institutions of western culture, including the church, are inheritors of the racism which flourished for more than 300 years in Europe and America and continues today in many manifest and latent forms.

Christianity and Anti-Semitism

Although, the word "anti-Semitism"[11] is of nineteenth-century coinage, it is an old and always present form of discrimination in which ethnic origin and religion interconnect. Discrimination based on the theory of racial superiority was used to justify the civil and religious persecution of Jews. With the rise and domination of Christianity throughout the Western world, discrimination against Jews on religious grounds[12] became universal and systematic and social anti-Judaism made its appearance. Jews were segregated in ghettos, required to wear identifying marks or garments and were economically crippled by the imposition of restrictions on their

9 C. Hallinan, Divide and Conquer as Imperial Rulers Foreign Policy in Focu (para 24). Retrieved from http:/fpil.org/divide-and-conquer-as-imperial-rulers/.

10 This colonial practice is described in *The Creation of Tribalism in Southern Africa* (Los Angeles: Univ. of California Press, 1991),

11 The term is used to include speech and behavior that is derogatory to the people of Jewish origin.

12 For a detailed discussion on religious and theological roots of anti-Semitism refer RoseMary Ruether, 'The Christian Roots of Anti-Semitism,' in *Theology and Racism 1: The Bible, Racism and Anti-Semitism* ed. by Kenneth Leech (n.p: Race, Pluralism and the Community Group of the Board for Social Responsibility of the Church of England, 1985), 15-23.

business activities. Forced baptism, public burning of the Talmud and other Jewish books, together with many massacres, especially during the Crusades, remain an indelible part of the history of the Jews in Europe. Thus,

> through a combination of official inferiorization from the Church and Christian state and hatred whipped up by popular preachers, the ghetto was gradually shaped around the Jewish community in Christendom until practices such as the 'Jewish badge' and ghetto walls became institutions by the late middle ages. The status of a Jew as a person without honour or civil rights in Christian society was to last until modern times and was swept away in Eastern Europe only by the Nazi Holocaust itself![13]

The reality of anti-Semitism is not peculiar to Europe, however. Today small groups of neo-Nazis and white supremacists in different parts of the world have been primarily responsible for anti-Semitic propaganda. In several countries throughout the world, synagogues have been attacked or burnt. Jewish community buildings and clubs have been subject of anti-Semitic graffiti and pictures of swastikas. Desecrations of Jewish cemeteries have occurred in many countries and Jews have met with physical violence, some of which has been fatal.

The Jewish community has historically been a frequent target. Many explanations of the phenomenon of anti-Semitism have been advanced. "One theory suggests that anti-Semitism is nurtured in periods of social and economic instability and crisis. Frustrations engendered during such periods are deflected on to scapegoats."[14] The escalation of the Israeli-Palestinian conflict and the way some people perceived it or chose to depict it had an aggravating effect on the resurgence of anti-Semitism, especially in some European countries.

---

13 Ibid., 21-22.

14 Jews as scapegoats was suggested by Dr. Hans in his paper on the subject of anti-Semitism, Geneva, 2002, 1.

Islamophobia and Discrimination against the Arabs

It is necessary to acknowledge and to confront the visible development of anti-Semitism and discrimination against Muslims and persons of Arab descent in various parts of the world today. This escalation obstructs the possibility of people who belong to those communities to live their lives as Jews and Muslims according to their cultural and religious tradition. There is an emergence of stereotyping, hostile acts and violence against these communities. In several cases their situation is aggravated by the fact that they have a specific racial or ethnic origin. The official governments' report of the 2001 UN World Conference against Racism, Racial Discrimination, Xenophobia and Related Intolerance recognized this by acknowledging "with deep concern the increase in anti-Semitism and Islamophobia"[15] and the emergence of racial and violent movements based on racism and discriminatory ideas against Jewish, Muslim and Arab communities.

The scapegoat explanation applies also to the understanding of the contemporary development of violence against foreigners in different parts of the world, relating also to the situation of foreigners of Jewish or Muslim religious affiliation.

The phenomenon of discrimination against Muslims is not new. The derogatory image of Muslims and Islam began as early as the Crusades during the 11th to the 13th centuries when Christians, clergy, lay people and armies, marched to Palestine in order to free Jerusalem and the Holy Land from Islamic influence and authority.[16]

The United Nations Human Rights Commission's Special Rapporteur on Religious Intolerance, Mr. Abdelfattah Amor, in his various reports point to the different forms of discrimination on the basis of religion.[17] These include discrimination and xenophobia

---

15 See the Declaration of World Conference Against Racism, Racial Discrimination, Xenophobia and Related Intolerance, Durban, South Africa, 31 August-8 September, 2001, 61.

16 Dr. Tom J. Rees, The Story of the First Crusade, http//www.brighton73. Freeserve.co.uk/first crusade

17 See special Rapporteur on Religious Intolerance, Mr. Abdel Fattah Amor, reports http:/www.unhchr/Huridocda/Huridoca.nsf.

directed at North African or Arab nationals or persons of Arab or North African descent in western Europe and the United States; Turkish nationals or those of Turkish origin in Germany and Austria; discrimination against Palestinians in Israel; discrimination and intolerance affecting the Muslim community, and particularly Muslims of Indian and Pakistani origin in the United Kingdom.

Referring to the United States, the Special Rapporteur says that: "manifestations of racism and xenophobia against Arabs are increasingly accompanied by a form of 'Islamophobia'. It is therefore difficult to separate acts of racial discrimination from acts of religious intolerance, as each may reinforce or encourage the other."[18]

The September 11th destruction of the twin towers of the World Trade Centre and the attacks in the Pentagon in Washington D.C., have engendered prejudices and led to the stereotyping of all persons of Arab descent or of the Muslim faith. The United States "war against terrorism," in conjunction with stereotyping in mass media coverage, has been yet another element aggravating the situation in many parts of the world. Quite often the mass media have led viewers (listeners, readers) to believe that all such persons were real or potential terrorists.

Ecumenical Involvement in Combating Racism

The rise of the ecumenical movement coincided with, and influenced, world-wide efforts to struggle against racism and white racism in particular. As early as 1924, J. H. Oldham challenged the churches to end the vicious circles of injustice and racial discrimination.[19] Since then, but mainly after the World War II, there have been many unambiguous statements which condemned racism as a denial of Christian faith and as incompatible with the Gospel. "Between 1925 and 1968 some 30 statements of this kind were made by ecumenical gatherings and hundreds more have been made by many different churches."[20] If racism could be eradicated by passing church

---

18 Ibid.

19 See J. H. Oldham, *Christianity and the Race Problem* (London: SCM Press, 1924).

20 C. Duraisingh, *Racism in Theology: Theology Against Racism* (Geneva: WCC, 1975), 4.

resolutions it would have disappeared long ago. Yet, inspite of all these statements and the substantial agreement among the churches which they represent, racism remains as deeply entrenched as ever.

An ecumenical consultation summed up reflections on racism in the following ways:

1. Racism is present whenever persons, even before they are born, because of their race, are assigned to a group severely limited in their freedom of movement, their choice of work, their places of residence and so on.
2. Racism is present whenever groups of people, because of their race, are denied effective participation in the political process, and so are compelled to obey the edicts of government which they were allowed to have no part in choosing.
3. Racism is present whenever racial groups within a nation are excluded from the normal channels available for gaining economic power, through denial of educational opportunities and entry into occupational groups.
4. Racism is present whenever the policies of a nation-state ensure benefits for that nation from the labour of racial groups (migrant or otherwise), while at the same time denying to such groups commensurate participation in the affairs of the nation-state.
5. Racism is present whenever the identity of persons is denigrated through stereotyping of racial or ethnic groups in text books, cinema, mass media, interpersonal relations and other ways.
6. Racism is present whenever people are denied equal protection of the law, because of race, and when constituted authorities of the state use their powers to protect the interests of the dominant group at the expense of the powerless.
7. Racism is present whenever groups or nations continue to profit from regional and global structures that are historically related to racist presuppositions and actions.[21]

---

21 Ibid., 3-4.

The WCC, as the largest ecumenical body, from its very inception, has been deeply conscious of the roles played by Christians and churches in fomenting anti-Semitism during the period of the Holocaust. From the time of its first Assembly in 1948 it has consistently condemned anti-Semitism and other forms of discrimination or intolerance based on race, religion or national origin. At the fourth Assembly at Uppsala 1968, WCC constituted the sub-division 'Programme to Combat Racism' to go beyond the resolutions and to make way for action oriented programme which, by its emphasis on projects and financial assistance, had underlined the churches' commitment to combat racism.[22]

Contemporary Situation

Towards the third quarter of the 20th century, in the US, various Christian-based white churches began to distance themselves from the racist rhetoric and teachings of their faith. The LDS Church, however, remained steadfast in its persistence of racist folklore well beyond the Civil Rights era. Though, the Church did eventually change its position on blacks in 1978, they actually did so with a generic message, which did not (and has yet to) address specifically their mistreatment of Blacks. While the Catholic Church and other Protestant based faiths—Episcopal Church, United Methodist Church, Southern Baptist, Lutheran—have since made peace with their racist past and issued public apologies for their role in slavery, Jim Crow racism, and their participation in the mistreatment of African Americans at the hands of misguided Christians.[23] The LDS Church remains unshakable, convinced that its policy was divinely sanctioned by God and that no such apology is needed. The colonial and white Reformed Church in South Africa had since the 1990s distanced itself from its earlier racist position but traces of it still linger.

Effects of traditional Christian attitudes to racial matters still continue today: they cannot be obliterated in a single generation. When Ugandan born John Sentanu was enthroned as Archbishop of

22 Ibid., 4.

23 http://racerelations.about.com/od/historyofracerelations/a/How-Four-Christian-Denominations-in-The -US-Atoned-For-Racism.htm

York in 2005 he received a hail of insulting racist letters some of them smeared with **excrement.** They presumably came from Anglicans, and possibly from other Christians, as non-Christians would not have reason to care. Sociological studies in Britain and the USA have demonstrated that Christians still tend to be more racially prejudiced than non-Christians. In a book comparing the results of studies concerning prejudice, the authors state that "The basic finding that church members are more prejudiced than non-members has been widely confirmed in American studies." According to these studies Roman Catholics were the most prejudiced major denomination in the US. Similar studies showed that Anglicans were the most prejudiced in Britain. In another study, religious orthodoxy was found to be positively correlated with belief in racial segregation.[24]

In many places throughout the world whites still go to one church, and blacks to a different one on the other side of town. This practice is largely responsible for the growth of separate white and black Churches. What Martin Luther King observed still holds true to a large extend, that the USA is most segregated at 11am on Sunday morning [when all good Christians are in their own racially segregated churches].

Since the end of the 1960's the only remaining avowed white supremacists in the world were Christians. The hard-core of white supremacists in South Africa are still strong Christians, as are those in other countries. In the UK the only political party that required members to be Christian was the British National Party. In America, Christians with traditional views kept alive the Ku Klux Klan. In the twenty first century, Christian Klan members are still engaging in activities such as arson attacks on non-white homes, churches,[25] and participating in anti-immigration marches.

Conclusion

The effort to overcome racism does in fact seem to have become an imperative which is broadly anchored in human consciences. "Any doctrine of superiority based on the difference between races is scientifically false, morally condemnable and socially unjust and

24 Nolan Kraszkiewics, Facebook post, March 30, 2013.

25 A recent example is the shooting at the Emanuel AME church at Charleston.

dangerous."[26] The Church's doctrine affirms it with no less vigour all racist theories are contrary to Christian faith and love. And yet, in sharp contrast to this growing awareness of human dignity, racism still exists and continually reappears in different forms. It is a thorn in humanity's co-existence. Everyone, therefore, must make efforts to heal it with great firmness and patience. Respect for every person and every race is respect for basic rights, dignity and fundamental equality. This does not mean erasing cultural differences. Instead it is important to educate to a positive appreciation of the complementary diversity of peoples. A well-understood pluralism resolves the problem of closed racism.

26 Para. 6 of the Preamble of the International Convention on the Elimination of all forms of Racial discrimination which was adopted on December 21, 1965.

9

Interrogating the Role of Media for or Combating Racism

An Advocacy towards Peaceful Co-existence in the Society

A. Temjen Jamir[1]

Introduction

During the last many centuries, the human communities have been witnessing and experiencing the menace of racism in the society. In this connection, mass media have played and will continue to play a crucial role in perpetuating racism in terms of creating racial division between rich and poor, majority and minorities, white and black, master and servant, etc., in the society. On this racial line of division and segregation, the ethnic minorities, poor people and weaker sections of the society are being projected through the media as second class citizens, "others," problem makers and vicious, anti-social groups, etc. As a result, they are being victimized with all forms of oppressions, suppressions, exploitations and discriminations that disturb peaceful co-existence with one another in the society. At this point, it provokes our thoughts and moves us to carefully look into the media being used by the dominant class of the society for racial

1 Rev. Dr. A. Temjen Jamir is the Associate Professor in the Department of Communication and the Academic Dean at the Clark Theological College, Mokokchung, Nagaland.

discrimination and oppression of the weaker sections of the society. Further, it will also help us to envision as how the media can be used to combat racism in the society in order to promote peaceful coexistence with one another in the society.

1. Media Power and Racism

Our colloquial discourse on racism is closely connected with the power of media and the political economy of communication in the society. At this point, the pertinent question is that, 'Who owns and controls the media? Since the Mass media are powerful means of communication, those who own and control the media, they control the people and the society; they also control the economic and political power in the society. According to Karl Marx, society has two classes: the exploited or working class and the exploiters or owners of the means of production. Communication media are being owned by the ruling capitalist class and operate them in the interest of that class.[2] In fact, the question of power is fundamental to Marxism and Marxist interpretation of mass media that media are ultimately instruments of control by a ruling capitalist class.[3] At this juncture, racism serves as a means to subdue the working class or the weaker sections of the people in the society. In 1980s, Michael Reich propounded the Segmentation Theory or the Divide and Rule that explained racism from an economic point of view. Consequently, the exploiters attempts to use any means to: (1) suppress higher wages among the exploited class, (2) weaken the bargaining power of the working class, often by attempting to split it along racial lines, (3) promote prejudices, (4) segregates the black community, (5) ensure that the elite benefit the creation of stereotypes and racial prejudices against the black community.[4] Racism is also inextricably linked with socio-economic factors, and frequently reflects underlying

---

2 Murdock, G. and Golding, P., "Capitalism, Communication and Class Relations," In *Mass Communication and Society*. Edited by J. Curran et al. (eds). London: Edward Arnold, 1977, pp. 10-45.

3 Denis McQuail, *Mass Communication Theory: An Introduction*, Second Edition. London: SAGE Publications, 1987, pp. 82-83.

4 Stephen Balkaran, "Mass Media and Racism." In www.yale.edu/ypo/articles/oct99.html 29-10-2015.

socio-economic inequalities. The increasing globalization of the marketplace and development of new technologies has the potential to maintain these divisions in societies (particularly for education poor groups), as well as to create new patterns of exclusion and marginalization. In this rapid period of economic globalization and transnational restructuring we have also seen a growing sense of marginalization and social disenfranchisement amongst groups which had in the past identified themselves as part of the 'mainstream' or dominant forces of society.[5]

In this relation the report of the Bellagio Consultation on the World Conference Against Racism states that ultimately, racism is a tool to gain and maintain power. 'A significant cause (and effect) of racism in the world today stems from colonialism and slavery, the results of which include the often near-total exploitation, dispossession and dislocation of certain groups of people (or of peoples); misappropriation of their lands and resources; and denial of their very humanity. The continuing legacy of colonialism and slavery is evidenced in many places and in many ways, some more obvious than others.'[6]

In fact, the media of communication are being owned and controlled by the dominant class of those rich, elites and media professionals. Thus, they decide the message and set the agenda[7] on their favour in the media in order to further suppress, segregate and overpower the exploited class of the people in the society. The powerful media of communication are used to filter information and distort truth, thus, the audience tend to perceive certain issues as more important than the other issues because media concentrate

5 Combating Racism in Australia: A Discussion Paper by HREOC for the World Conference Against Racism. www. Humanrights.gov.au 31-10-2015.

6 Report of the Bellagio Consultation on the World Conference Against Racism. Bellagio, 24-28 January 2000, p. 3.

7 The agenda setting theory of mass media, propounded by Shaw and McCombs, hold that mass media do suggest to us which ideas, topics or information we are to think about or topics for which we will want to gather further information. The agenda setting hypothesis is that when a topic is potentially interesting to an audience, it attracts the attention of the audience to the mass media. Frederic Williams, *The New Communications*, III Edition. Belmont: Wedsworth Publishing Company, 1992, p. 154.

only on the few subjects they want audience to see and discuss. Mass media are often seen as bias in being selective on reporting issues and tend to amplify certain issues or distort events because of various factors such as political reasons or for commercial purpose.

There is also a higher tendency for headlines stories with racial dimensions as it usually creates much more upheaval within the community demanding justice. Ethnic minorities, immigrants, refugees become main topics of news especially when they are associated with alleged problems or menaces, such as deviance, drugs, crime and terrorism, economic or financial scarcity, unemployment, etc. However, their contributions to the economy, culture, etc., are seldom highlighted or ignored.[8] The press can play a vital role in the reproduction of or struggle against racism. In this connection, Van Dijk states that a vast amount of research in many countries has demonstrated, again and again, that on the whole, the press is rather part of the problem of racism, than part of its solution. This is more explicitly the case for the right-wing popular press, such as The Sun in the UK or Bild Zeitung in Germany, but also applies to quality newspapers, and not only those of the Right. Many studies show that the major problems of the press that contribute to the reproduction of prejudiced beliefs, and hence indirectly to the reproduction of racism as a system of inequality. This leads to biased news gathering in terms of paying less attention for or reliance on non-white groups, persons or organizations as credible sources, experts, etc. – even when these are available. This also leads to biased citation patterns in citing only white elite sources as reliable sources, thereby publicly marginalizing ethnic leaders and experts.[9] In the present European context, White groups dominate ethnically or racially different groups by the exercise of various types of physical, social or symbolic control. Thus, the minority groups are systematically, although often

8 Teun A. Van Dijk, "Racism. The Press and Freedom of Expression: A Summary of Ten Theses". In *Expert Seminar: Combating Racism While Respecting Freedom of Expression, Organized by European Commission Against Racism and Intolerance (ECRI)* Proceedings Strasbourg, 16-17 November 2006, July 2007, p. 32.

9 Teun A. Van Dijk, "Racism. The Press and Freedom of Expression: A Summary of Ten Theses." In *Expert Seminar: Combating Racism While Respecting Freedom of Expression, Organized by European Commission Against Racism and Intolerance (ECRI)* Proceedings Strasbourg, 16-17 November 2006, July 2007, p. 31.

indirectly and subtly, denied equal rights, that is, equal access to material or cultural resources, and equal opportunities in housing, work, health care or education.[10]

New Media as Public Space for Racial Discourse

Today, as we live in the age of Information Communication Technology, along with the improvement in the quality of life, access to different types of media is no longer limited to the rich and powerful. Mass media now serves as an important platform for people to gain knowledge and share information with the world. However, this convenience also has its disadvantages as people grew to heavily rely on media to gain new knowledge and information, so much to an extend it shape their mentalities and perceptions.[11] As such, accessibility to media contents especially, those information with racial slur or racial discourse can influence people to a large extend. In this connection, Social Media can be seen as computer-mediated tools such as *MySpace*, *whatsapp*, *Twitter*, *Facebook*, etc., are the networking sites where users can create their own account and expand their network by connecting with friends all over the world. Social media are the collective of online communications channels dedicated to community-based input, interaction, content-sharing and collaboration. Social Media can be used for both good and bad purposes depending upon the users. Chris Hoenig states that racist and derogatory messages are posted on Twitter at a rate of about 10,000 tweets per day, or roughly seven tweets every minute, according to a report from a British think tank. In addition, slurs and other racially charged terms are being thrown about in an increasingly casual manner on social media.[12] In fact, misusing of this space by posting racist and derogatory messages can bring huge damage to the society.

10 Teun A. van Dijk, "Mediating Racism: The Role of the Media in the Reproduction of Racism." 29 10 2015.

11 http://www.mediapromotes racism.wordpress.com 'Media and Racism: A deeper in-sight of the Role of Media in Pormoting Racism.' 30-10-2015.

12 http://www.shutterstock.com/pic-154181867/stock-photo-brussels-september-twitter-is-going-public-on-september-in-brussels.html?src=csl_recent_image-1 30-10-2015.

2. Perpetuating Racism through Media

As mentioned earlier, racism has existed throughout human history based on the belief that a particular race or person is less humankind because of different outlook, skin color, language, culture, traditions, place of birth, etc. According to Yasmin Jiwani, the ethnic minorities or the marginalized people or people of colour tend to be absent from the media in general. However, they are obviously present in stories and incidents with crime, stealing, anti-social problems.[13]

Racism in the early 20th century was largely between the blacks and whites in America, but today it has evolved and expanded among many different cultures in countries throughout the world. Racism is being defined as the prejudice or discrimination directed against someone of a different race based on such a belief. It is a common phenomenal happening around the globe. The problems that happen from racism can be catastrophic. For instance, race riots in Los Angeles in 1992 as a result of severe racial dispute. Due to the growing media influence, racism has evolved from "black and white" in the past to the multi-cultural issue in our times. Racism is a global issue faced by many countries. It is identified as a serious issue that can cause social unrest and moral panic in society. Here, the media also refused to search and explain the underlying factors and problems behind protest, violence and destruction, which indicates the bias attitude and treatment of media towards the minority Black Community.[14]

Racism also causes hate-crimes such as murder or racial harassment. For instance, in India on 29th January 2014, Nido Taniam (19) son of Arunachal Pradesh MLA, was mercilessly beaten up by two shopkeepers Wednesday afternoon following a row over his appearance and clothing. He died on 30 January 2014 at a hospital Thursday. In this connection, activist and people from the Northeast India condemned and termed it as a "racial attack." However, prior to the post-mortem, the *Asian Age* newspaper wrote on February 4

---

13 Yasmin Jiwani, "Racism and the Media Taxonomy Categories: Anti-racism Theory". http://www.stopracism.ca/content/racism-and-media 26-10-2015.

14 Stephen Balkaran, "Mass Media and Racism". www. Yale.edu/ypq/articles/oct99.html 29-10-2015.

saying Nido Taniam died of drug overdose.[15] Media often perpetuate racism by hiding and twisting the truth against the minorities group and present the story with negative connotation using the terms "drug abusers," "criminals," and "law breakers."

2.1. Normalization of Racism through Stereotyping

Stereotyping is one very common and effective way in which racism is perpetuated. Racism is being exercised constantly by mass media which might influence the audience's way of stereotyping groups and also give them the impression that racism is common and normalized. The media uses stereotypes as a shorthand method of defining characters in ways that are easy for people to identify and categorize. What these stereotypes all have in common is that they reduce to a one-sided, superficial and exaggerated depiction the real variety, depth and complexity of a people. The media today is more sensitive to issues of culture and gender than it once was, but the creation and perpetuation of common misconceptions about groups of people continues.[16] According to Cultivation theory, media provide their audience a common perception and value based on what is portrayed on the TV, it could be due to the audiences constant exposure to racist context in everyday's media contact, thus they tend to get the impression that racism is normal. If a particular media portrays a specific ethnic group in a negative light, then it can result in creating anxiety against that specific group of people. For example, the reports on black people since the slave trade, how they represent black people and constantly associate them with terms like crime, drugs, and rape.[17] This tends to leave a negative impression of the certain group in the audience's mind and they are more likely to associate their future experiences based on their impression. Thus, when a particular message or idea is constantly disseminated with negative connotation about a particular race, then that will give a wrong impression to the audience that they are rather weak

15 ww.aljazeera.com/indepth/features/2014/02/voices-from-india-northeast-.html 28-10-2015.

16 www.racist – stereotypes.com 13-10-2015.

17 http://www.mediapromotes racism.wordpress.com 'Media and Racism: A deeper in-sight of the Role of Media in Pormoting Racism'. 30-10-2015.

and problematic in the society. For example, this falls in line with stereotyping that 'the North-eastern women are morally loose and easy to get.'[18] This kind of message will not only damage the identity and dignity of the women from the North-eastern regions but also will convey a bias and negative image about the women in particular, the people from the regions in general.

2.2. Segregation of Ethnic Minorities or Ethnic Groups through Racial Prejudices

Racial prejudices can be seen as being pre-judging others on racial lines that aimed at segregating and isolating them dominant class of the society. Media play a vital role in positioning and representing peoples who are different from what is considered acceptable in the society. Media construct and convey negative signs and symbols with meanings of threats, incursion and pollution. In order to combat racism, it is important to understand its root ideological segregation and separation on racial line. There is always an "us" and a "them," a "self" and an "other." In U.S. national ideology, the other has variously consisted of savage Indians, baby-killing Germans, fiendish Japanese, the Evil Empire of world communism, and, now, the Green Menace of Islam and the terrorist Arabs. In this connection, they spread misinformation about a group of people to present them as the other; increase the prejudice about them; enact a policy that affects them and is itself directly supported by the growing racism; and then the policy itself becomes utilized in the misinformation media game.[19] Ethnic minorities and people who are different outlook are positioned as "others" "They" are the criminals, "they" are dirty, untidy, "they" cause trouble and diseases. "They" have to be contained in a separate area away from "civilized" society. "They" are not like one of "us."[20] Such deprecating and offensive phrases and words can rather build walls and barriers between people of different

---

18 ww.aljazeera.com/indepth/features/2014/02/voices-from-india-northeast-.html 28-10-2015.

19 Rania Masri, "Combating Racism: Only Together – with Our Arms Locked". In *International Socialist Review* Issue 19, July-August 2001. p. 32.

20 Yasmin Jiwani, "Racism and the Media Taxonomy Categories: Anti-racism Theory, http://www.stopracism.ca/content/racism-and-media 26-10-2015.

race, instead of building peace and harmony with one another in the society. In this connection, Teun A. van says that White journalists primarily write as White ingroup members, and hence represent ethnic minority groups in terms of 'them.' Since, ethnic minorities are also predominantly working class, are less organized in powerful institutions, and have little political influence, the two dimensions of race and class combined produce social cognitions and therefore social practices among journalists that tend to ignore these outgroups or to represent them in a consistently negative framework.[21]

The dominant class of society has often intention to suppress and discriminate the immigrants and minority groups in the society so that these oppressed people do not progress and develop to the full as human kind which can be seen as the violation of human rights. In this relation, Phurpa Tsering, from the Northeast India, said that "Men are portrayed as drug addicts, drop outs, good for nothing, scumbags. These events, like Nido's killing, rape cases are very polarizing. It makes you very conscious of your race. Who you are? What you are? This will result in isolation."[22] This indicates that the people from the Northeast India are being treated as outsiders or others, not as Indian citizens. As a result, they are being victimized by racist slur and discriminations. At this point, I want to raise a pertinent question, as people from the North-east India, are we free from racial prejudices? Or do we also practice racial prejudices towards other people from other the States? For instance, if we call the plain people from other States of India, coming to our land for government job, business and trading purposes, the construction labours, etc., "Tzumai," "Beharis," or any other expression assigned with negative connotations may refer to as "outsiders," "others," and "they are not one of us," it may rather promote discrimination of these people which need be checked and condemned, if it prevails in the regions.

---

21 Teun A. van Dijk, "Mediating Racism: The Role of the Media in the Reproduction of Racism". 29-10-2015.

22 ww.aljazeera.com/indepth/features/2014/02/voices-from-india-northeast--.html 28-10-2015.

2.3. Use of Racist Language

Racism is being perpetuated increasingly due to misuse of language. Racist and intolerant attitude has been increasingly developed; criminalization is being taking place because of the misuse of language, words, signs and symbols in a multi-cultural and religious society. All the racist language and words are attached with negative connotations and racial discriminations against another ethnic group of people. Calling people from the North-east India 'Chinese,' 'Koreans,' 'Japanese,' 'Nepalese,' 'Chinkis,' 'Momos,' 'Bahadurs,' 'Chichi Chu Chu,' and any other derogatory remarks relating to race, culture, identity, or physical appearances are unacceptable and can be termed as dehumanising attitude and gesture towards these people. Phrases like, Are you from Nepal or China? Do you eat snakes, dogs, human meat, dry fish, akhuni, etc., are encapsulated with racial discrimination, which may be followed by physical assault. For this reason, in India the north-eastern community protested and campaigned for an anti-racism legislation. In this connection, we can hear the voices from the brothers and sisters of the North-east India, "We recognize that there is racism in India not only against northeast people but also against south Indians, adivasis (tribals). That is why we want a cohesive and comprehensive law that addresses racism in the country."[23] In this regard, the Bezbaruah Committee[24] recommended a provision in Section 153 of IPC to provide for imprisonment up to five years with a fine to "whoever, by words, either spoken or written or by signs or by visible representations or otherwise attempts or promotes to attempt on the ground of race or place of origin or such other grounds relating to racial feature of to racial behavior and culture or racial customs or participates in such activity intending to use criminal force or violence.."[25] Using racist language and words

23 ww.aljazeera.com/indepth/features/2014/02/voices-from-india-northeast--.html 28-10-2015.

24 The Bezbaruah Committee, headed by M.P. Bezbaruah, Member, North Eastern Council, was set up in February 2014 after the death of Nido Tania, a 19-year-old student fromArunachal Pradesh, who died in Delhi on January 29, 2014.

25 "Law Against Race Attacks Soon" In *Nagaland Post*. Vol. XXV. No. 72. Dimapur, Tuesday, February 17, 2015, p. 1.

against another ethnic group of people is detrimental and dangerous. It does not bring any good but only harm to others which demands justice through legal process and collective coordinated efforts.

3. Combating Racism: Towards Peaceful Co-existence in the Society

One of the important roles of the media of communication is to provide the right and unbiased information to the audience; however it has been curtailed by the rich and ruling class of the society for maximization of profit (economic and political power) at the expense of the poor and minority groups of people in the society. At this point, racism has been seen as a tool at the hands of the dominant class of the society to crush and overpower the minority and weaker sections of the society. Thus, justice is being denied. As a result, peaceful co-existence with one another is being disturbed. When our brothers and sisters are harassed, exploited, discriminated and assaulted, in such a situation we cannot expect peace, instead experiencing of psychological fear, terror and hopelessness may be haunting them miserably that may destroy their lives apart. In such a situation, advocating peace and justice is an inevitable task and paramount important for all the peace loving people in the society. Thus, our commitment to combat racism must check and voice against all forms of racial discriminations, crime and actions that are being promoted through media of communication, and to support peacebuilding initiatives through the media of communication.

1. Community media which are available within the community can be used as a means to promote the participation of ethnic minority groups in society. It will enable them voice out their needs and concerns on a common platform. In this relation, complementing the mainstream media, they can play a mediating role between communities and provide access to minority networks and to alternative sources of information. Increasing the representation of minority groups in the mainstream media can be encouraged which does not mean that journalists with minority backgrounds should

only report on minority issues, but that they can bring in a special perspective on many issues.[26]

2. The Internet and social media can be helpful tools for combating racism and racial discrimination. Information communication technologies like the Internet offer great potential for reaching and connecting communities in terms of sharing proper information and knowledge with one another. New technologies promise new ways to remove barriers, including those that result from racism, racial discrimination, xenophobia and related intolerance.[27] People can chat and surf the world, learning about one another and familiarizing themselves with different cultures, languages and perspectives. However, the Net also presents serious risks such as greater access to racial hatred material can recruit new members and distribute hate propaganda. In regard to the media and Internet we need to educate people as how to maintain and keep at pace the right to freedom of expression with responsibility so that they may not become instrument for racism but to be motivated to combating racism.

3. Racism is learnt through racist discourse and communication in the society. The problem here is not only open and obvious racism as advocated by tassel groups, but mainstream racism that is conveyed in society by writers, professors, journalists, editors, politicians, text book writers, teachers etc. They may contribute to perpetuating racism and racial discrimination in society and therefore, they should also be part of the solution when it comes to combating racist discourse.

4. Reporting diversity is a skill that can be acquired to become aware of racial prejudices, to manage them and get rid of them, which is indeed a very difficult task. Therefore, time to time, training and educational measures should be imparted to all who engage themselves in the profession of journalism including those established media professionals. Further, educating the general public to recognize racism, racial discrimination, xenophobia and

26 Combating Racism in Australia: A Discussion Paper by HREOC for the World Conference Against Racism. www. Humanrights.gov.au 31-10-2015.

27 Combating Racism in Australia: A Discussion Paper by HREOC for the World Conference Against Racism.

related intolerance and to understand their impacts is also frequently suggested as an important way to prevent the recurrence of these problems. Educational systems build attitudes and shape behaviors. Educative measures to combat racism could take many forms, ranging from the formal education process to broader community education about racism.[28]

Conclusion

Communication is a spiritual exercise, brings people together for interaction and fellowship with one another. It aims at building community and unity with one another instead of creating divisions among human community, enhances participation and affirms justice and challenges injustice.[29] Our efforts to combat racism and rejection of racial discrimination are not only a moral issue but it is basic to our commitment to engage ourselves in our locality and region, and anywhere, when the tasks and duty demanded our response and action. Thus, through our coordinated efforts and initiatives may be able to promote a community where the oppressed and exploited class of the society may experience just peace and peaceful co-existence with one another.

---

28 Combating Racism in Australia.

29 Communication For all: Sharing World Association for Christian Communication's Principles, pp. 1-2.

10

Communication and Racism Communication A Cure or Curse

Butesen Ozukum[1]

Introduction

Communication has played a vital role in the very existence and development of human kind from the very beginning. Looking at it from a theological perspective, communication began with God (John 1:1). The purpose of creating commonness and solidarity is in the very nature of communication. However, far from its very purpose of creating oneness, with the rapid developments taking place in communication and information technology, communication today tends to reinforce more divisions than unity, it's widening the gap between the rich and the poor rather than bridging it, it is consolidating oppression, and distorting reality in order to maintain systems of domination and subject the silenced masses to media manipulation. Yet, in with all its misinterpreted flaws, communication still stands strong as one of God's greatest gifts to humanity. Without communication we cannot be truly human, nor can we enjoy living together and coexisting together with all our cultural differences as individuals, as groups and as communities.

Racism is a reality in our society that affects each individual in one way or the other – either as victims or as perpetuators. The

1 Mr. Butesen Ozukum is the Communication Officer at NEICORD (North East India Committee on Relief and Development), Guwahati.

nature of how racism takes place and how we interpret it becomes so complicated that we find it difficult to actually define it or draw a line as to what can be or cannot be considered as racism. Decade after decade people and different interests groups have tried to find ways to do away with it, with little or no achievements. If commonness, oneness, unity, peaceful coexistence, etc., is in the very nature of communication, can it be a cure for racism? Or has the purpose of communication been misinterpreted with selfish interests to perpetuate more differences between and within individuals and communities, thus becoming a curse?

Theories of Communication

The role that communication plays on the concerns of racism has its roots in a set of theories that have evolved under different developmental stages of Communication based on different prevailing sets of conditions and values. Despite numerous theories of communication that have emerged under different given circumstances, we will briefly look into a few important theories that have shaped the way of how individuals and society interpret and use communication media:

Authoritarian Theory

According to this theory, mass media (or even new media[2]), though not under the direct control of the state, had to follow its bidding. This theory stemmed from the authoritarian philosophy of Plato who thought that the state was safe only in the hands of a few wise men.[3]

The result of this theory was the advocacy to promote absolute dictatorship of media. It gave rise to the prompt obedience to a superior hierarchical structure and punishment for those who did not follow the censorship rules, which was justified on the ground

---

2 Just as the term 'mass media' is used to generally mean the newspaper, radio and television, the term 'new media' is used to mean different media of communication through internet media. Social networking sites are examples of new media.

3 Theory of Communication. www.peoi.org

that the state always took precedence over the individual's right to freedom of expression.

We are witnesses to authoritarian means of control over media even in democratic set ups where freedom of expression for individuals are stated only in paper. The emergence of different new media technologies seems to somehow give every individual the freedom to express freely. However, different psychological fears are implanted already in the hearts of people through different authorities in control thus restricting their freedom to express.

Libertarianism or Free Press Theory

This theory emerged based on the emphasis to the right of an individual, where the state was thought of as the major source of interference on the rights of the individual and his/her properties. This theory dates back to as early as the 17th century after the Guttenberg Revolution made it possible to print several copies of booklets and pamphlets at a faster and cheaper rate.

It is based on this theory that in 1789, France, in their Declaration of the Rights of Man, wrote, 'Every citizen may speak, write and publish freely.' This theory gave rise to the idea of a free marketplace of ideas. George Orwell defined the Free Press Theory as "allowing people to say things you do not want to hear."[4] What this theory offered was power without responsibility and today our society is witness to this theory of communication, especially with regard to the use of different social networking media.

Social Responsibility Theory

This theory emerged as a direct response to the free press theory. Proponents to this theory advocated for the need of a social responsibility on the concept of free press thus giving rise to the Social Responsibility Theory. This theory is said to have been initiated in the United States by the Commission of the Freedom of Press in 1949 on the basis of their finding that the free market approach to press freedom has only increased the power of a single class and has not served the interest of the whole community.

---

4 Ibid.

With rapid developments taking place in the world of communication media, especially with the development of radio and television media, society was in search of a theory that would provide some means of accountability in the use of media. The social responsibility theory rightly advocated some obligation on the part of the media to society. We see the application of this theory in the production of different media products such as censorship regulations, where self regulation, state regulation, and high professional standards are essential.

Democratic Participant Media Theory (Democratization of Communication)

This theory vehemently opposes the commercialization of modern media (mass media) and its top-down non-participant character. This theory gained more prominence after UNESCO's MacBride Commission submitted its report in 1980 which emphasized on the importance of receiving and communicating information as rights. The report detailed the inequalities existing in the flow of information between the North and the South, with the latter only on the receiving end and the former determining what information was best for the rest of the world.

This theory advocates the need for a balanced access and right to communicate. It proposes communication as the center of all relations by bringing a uniformed flow of information among people of both ends. The development of different social networking technologies somehow is an attempt of materializing this theory of Communication.

Communication: A Curse

Marshal McLuhan's prediction of a global village has become a reality where no one corner of the earth is hidden from the other. The rapid development in information technology has made it possible for people to connect with each other from the comforts of their own rooms. With wide open possibilities to be informed about any corner of the world, coupled by the increasing demand for resources and consumption patterns, people began to come out of their own communities in search of better opportunities. This process of coexistence slowly has created a friction and strain in the shifting social fabric as communities from different cultures, faiths and traditions adjust to living together. People in each community coexist under circumstances where traditional groups of people within communities feel a loss of self-confidence, and immigrant communities also feel that their way of life can be under threat.

Sadly, but true, communication media has also not been of much help in advocating commonness among people amidst all these social tensions based on one's culture and ethnicity. Beginning from one's own very home and community, stereotyping people based on their appearance, culture, religion, occupation, geographical background, etc., are developed. And these stereotyped messages are spread further through the powerful medium of different communication media.

Many newspapers, broadcasters, advertising agencies and other media outlets have failed to rise to the challenge of portraying the global social revolution. Instead of raising awareness and challenging ignorance, they stoke the fires of intolerance and racism. Radio and television media, which dominated communication media and took mass communication to its peaks, only reiterated what print media propagated, thus widening the gap between communities and cultures.

The unprecedented, rapid development of new communication and information technologies, or new media, such as the internet and social media, which was supposed to bridge the communication gap and bring about commonness among communities, has also just enabled wider dissemination of racist and xenophobic content that incites racial hatred and violence.

Therefore, we see that the different communication theories that were developed to monitor and ensure commonness, have failed in one way or the other to bridge the gap of differences between individuals and communities. The different theories though developed with certain set of values and conditions, with misinterpretations and misrepresentations, it has only served the purpose of the few in power. In this regard, communication rather becomes a curse that perpetuating more racial tensions among communities.

How then can Communication become a cure? Should another communication theory based on the social setting of racism help? What if it only works out for the influential few? Or is imposing rigorous legal and policy efforts at regional and national levels to address the spread of racial, ethnic, and xenophobic hatred, especially through the internet and social media, the solution? There are already strong legislations enacted in many states to combat racism and ethnic hatred through any given media, whether mass media or new media. But how far have these legislations been helpful in bringing about a solution to the issue? We are yet to ascertain its results.

Communication from a Christian Perspective

Jesus' call and commission is all about the Good News – hearing the Good News, living by it and witnessing to it, is the basic calling of all Christians today.[5] It is a divine call for Christians, a divine communication which entails self-sacrifice and renunciation. Christ's own communication was an act of self-giving. He emptied himself, taking the form of a servant (Phil. 2:7). The ministry of Christ was to all people, taking up the cause of the materially poor, the mentally ill, the outcasts of society, the powerless and the oppressed. In the same way, as Christians, communication from our perspective should be about act of love which liberates all who take part in it.

If the Gospel is about being Good News for the poor and oppressed, then it needs to be constantly reinterpreted from the perspectives of the poor and oppressed. This challenges church hierarchies to disassociate themselves from the power structures which keep the poor and oppressed in a position of subservience. In this sense, the Good News for the poor embodies genuine reconciliation by means of which the dignity of all people can be reaffirmed.[6]

As Christians, we accept the sovereignty of Christ. Therefore, our communication should communicate the Kingdom of God rather than division in the society. Our communication should promote the central values of the Kingdom of God which are

5 Christian Principles of Communication. www.rjionline.org

6 Ibid.

reconciliation, equality, justice, freedom, harmony, peace, and love, rather than destroying it.

In short, Communication from a Christian perspective is about witnessing God's transforming power in all areas of life. Communication therefore can become a cure when we let our own respective communication theories to be shaped by certain Christian principles.

Communication: A Cure

Aware of the fact that different communication media are dividing and isolating people from each other, rather than uniting people towards common interest, the World Association for Christian Communication (WACC) developed a few guiding principles of Communication. These principles are expected to challenge Christians to disassociate themselves from power structures and promote genuine reconciliation through which the dignity of all people can be reaffirmed.

Genuine communication dismantles barriers of gender, race, class, nation, power, wealth, etc., and promotes justice, peace, and oneness. If Communication has to become a cure for racism in any form, then as Christians our Communication and its use should be shaped and influenced by the following set of Christian Principles.[7]

1. *Communication is a Spiritual Exercise*

As Christians, Jesus becomes our model for communication. In Jesus, God became one with humankind and experienced the marvelous intensity of human relationships. In Jesus, God became part of human history and affirmed the essential value of community and culture. Jesus lived out compassion for the poor, the sick and the excluded, and he challenged the powerful to serve those in need. In Jesus, God experienced the brokenness and pain produced by injustice. In Jesus, God lifted up the hope of healing and fulfillment, of abundant life for all.

All the values reflected by God through Jesus are not values that are restricted to Christian tradition alone. They are common to

7 The Christian Principles are excerpts from WACC's Core identity. "Communication for All". www.waccglobal.org

all faiths. Our interpretation of communication should be shaped by this principle – a communication that does not immortalize insolence but rather a communication through which we see, feel, and live out the values reflected by God through Jesus.

2. *Communication Builds and Shapes Community*

Communication is the invisible bond that holds communities together. This was the experience of the early Christian Church where "All the believers were together and had everything in common. They sold property and possessions to give to anyone who had need" (Acts 2: 44-45).

The life and existence any community is enriched by the open, honest and transparent dialogue about decisions and events affecting the lives of its members. This applies to any community whether it is a neighbourhood or village, a city, a religious community or a community of nations.

Relationships within a community can be developed and strengthened only when there is proper communication taking place among its members – a proper communication either through face-to-face conversations, or through different communication media run by and for its members, or social networking media that enable genuine participation in political, social and cultural questions relating to the common good.

Genuine communication calls for mutual accountability and building trust within members which in turn, strengthens community life. True communion is facilitated only when people join together to affirm their diversity, accept each other and commit to one another. It can enrich them and make them stronger. When our understanding of communication and its usage are guided by this principle, instead of enhancing division and spreading racist stereotypes through different communication media, we will find ourselves using communication to foster respect and acceptance of each other in the midst of all diversities.

3. *Communication Enhances Participation*

Participatory communication is open to dialogue where there is smooth exchange of ideas and acceptance of the transformation that emerges out of it. Inclusive communication does not seek simply to persuade people to accept pre-conceived ideas. Instead, it changes all participants where ideas become a communal work-in-progress. Participation also leads to transparency and mutual accountability as people come to understand their participation in the context of the well-being of their communities.

When communication is inclusive and invites participation, it makes worldviews and collective experiences richer and more vivid. More images, thoughts and points-of view are added to the public sphere.

Only when communication is participatory, it can empower individuals and communities, challenge authoritarian political, economic and cultural structures and help to build a more just and peaceful society. The danger of stereotypes is not only that they are untrue, but that they presuppose that one story is the only story, that one image becomes a token for all. Through participatory communication, stereotypes can be challenged as people use emerging technologies to exercise their right to communicate in the public space, uploading words and images instantly as events unfold.

4. *Communication Promotes Freedom and Demands Accountability*

The Christian tradition affirms that God invests all of humankind with freedom and dignity, and that God stands especially with the oppressed and marginalized, working through history for their liberation. God desires that all people be enabled to learn from and interpret their own reality

In today's world, communication must be lifted up as a fundamental human right and communicators called to practice an ethics of freedom and accountability. Freedom of expression must be respected and community groups assured access to technology and to media platforms. Educational curriculum must include media literacy programs. This is especially important in times of rapid social and technological change when traditional cultures need to develop constructive strategies for engaging external cultural influences. Together, such principles assure that a diversity of voices and images remain before the public and that the public can develop healthy criteria for discerning how those voices and images may contribute to the common good.

Many communities use different emerging communication technologies, together with more traditional media, as powerful tools with which they can demand accountability and celebrate their particular identities. In both rural and urban communities, information and communication technologies are being used for keeping in touch with friends and family, creative self-expression, commerce, accessing global culture, networking and advocacy.

This principle can help us challenge instances where different media and technology conglomerates, in partnership with government, practice surveillance and exercise unprecedented levels of control over citizens. It can furthermore help us in addressing interconnected monopolies, who control news, opinion and entertainment, often in the pursuit of narrow ideological agendas.

1. *Communication Celebrates Cultural Diversity*

Culture is what unites people as human beings, but it also unites people into groups to remain themselves aloft from other people groups. In today's world, it is increasingly important to understand and appreciate the similarities and differences between cultures. By appreciating similarities, people better understand their common humanity. By appreciating differences, people are able to affirm their self-worth in a global community that often trivializes notions of cultural identity.

Communication creates the symbolic environment in which identity, diversity and people's essential humanity co-exist. Genuine communication values people's dignity as human beings and their communities' cultures, especially in matters of language and faith. In this respect, and despite the homogeneity spawned by globalization, many people are rediscovering and reclaiming their cultural identity. This is vital when cultural memory, language, religion, gender, age, ethnicity or race, are denied by members of other cultural groups.

Communication is vital in creating meanings to different cultures. It can either sow understanding or misunderstanding, harmony or discord. That is why we see that people who wish to deny justice turn to communication to disempower and in contrast, those who wish to challenge injustice turn to communication to empower. Celebrating and defending cultures becomes a way of strengthening a community's sense of its inherent worth and identity. This principle can help us as Christians to nurture responsibility in creating meaningful and respectful images of the values and traditions that lie at the heart of other people's lives. It can further help us to avoid stereotypes, and strengthen inter-cultural and inter-religious understandings, thus promoting societies whose cultures live in peace together, affirming what each holds in common as well as what separates them.

2. *Communication Builds Connectedness*

Human beings are created to be in relationship with God, with each other and with the whole of creation. The whole created order bears God's image. For this reason, the well-being of all creation is a function of the well-being of each of its parts.

Today's globalized world is mired in multiple conflicts, ranging from ethnic and religious tensions, to disparities between rich and poor, to the challenges of climate justice. Contemporary media narratives, rooted in the conviction that polemic attracts bigger audiences, tend to exacerbate rather than assuage these tensions.

In today's world, developing communication skills that flow from an understanding of what all humans have in common – their inter-connectedness is urgent. Building connectedness through communication affirms the uniqueness of each person and each community: their faces, stories and experiences. In this way "the other" is not merely a set of data, but a being who is valued and who needs to be understood. This implies giving "others" the space to be themselves where they can feel free to say what they think.

Connectedness emphasizes human dignity, potential and creativity, as well as human finitude and vulnerability. It persuades us to seek new and vital forms of dialogue and action that transcend the boundaries of religion and ideology and that empower persons and communities. This principle can therefore help us in establishing relationships of loving care with each other and the wider creation.

3. *Communication Affirms Justice and Challenges Injustice*

In today's media world, a few powerful corporations and individuals decide whose voices are heard and what images are seen by the public, allowing them to shape policy, form public opinion and move people either towards war or peace. As Christians we can also announce the good news of how God is working in our midst to bend human history toward justice and peace. Such discernment takes on lasting meaning only when words are accompanied by action. To challenge injustice is to challenge the 'principalities and powers' which may even carry a high price.

Communication that affirms justice and challenges injustice serves truth and illuminates falsehood, since deception and half-truths threaten the common good. Denouncing the abuses of the powerful is necessary not because we are without fault, but because we hope to create community in a world where others seek to divide. Through this principle we can promote participation and freedom where others seek to enslave and to silence, and support and defend human dignity where others seek to destroy it. Knowing that by addressing power, we risk ourselves of being seduced by power itself, if we are to serve God, we must affirm justice and be willing to struggle against injustice.

Conclusion

In the light of all the discussions above, we affirm that communication embodies respect for the dignity, integrity, equality and freedom of all human beings and their communities. It is a powerful tool than can either bring about harmony or distort peace. We have also seen that communication in its own nature is vital to the very existence of humanity. People have used communication to create commonness and also communication to create division.

In the context of racism taking place at different levels, we are struggling with questions that search for answers to the subject of racism. Looking at the complexity of the subject, we also deem it almost impossible to pin out the answer to all our quests.

Without any hesitation, it is agreed that communication plays a vital role in propagating racism and we also have tried to apply WACC's guiding Christian principles as our guiding principles towards change. And yes, seems like it is also not impossible if we allow ourselves to be diligently guided by those principles as Christian communicators. At the end, the answer to all our struggles lies on how we individually interpret and use communication. Communication can be a curse and a cure as well.

Reference Materials

"Report of the Special Rapporteur on contemporary forms of racism, racial discrimination, xenophobia and related intolerance" http://www.ohchr.org

"Communication for all" http://www.waccglobal.org

"Theory of Communication." www.peoi.org

"Christian Principles of Communication." www.rjionline.org

"Social Communication in Christian Perspective" – FABC Roundtable on 'Social Communication in Religious Tradition of Asia'. Assumption University, Bangkok, October 3-7, 2005.

Racism and the Media. Yasmin Jiwani. www.stopracism.ca

Van Dijk, Teun A. "Mediating Racism, the Role of the Media in the Reproduction of Racism", in *Language, Power and Ideology*. Edited by J. Benjamin Publishing Company: Philadelphia, 1989.

11

Re-Imagining Gender and Racism through Prophetic Communication

Achemlu Ezung[1]

Introduction

Gendered racism is a form of oppression that occurs due to race and gender. It is perpetuated due to the prevalence of perceptions, stereotypes, and images of certain groups. Gendered racism also encompasses what is known as double hazard which can be defined as stereotypical portrayals of men and women of colour. Each woman is affected differently depending on her race, class, religion and geographical location, family of origin, school, system, ability and disability. Hence, her personal experiences are different and her expressions are different. There might be similarities but there is also diversity, variety, polarity and contradictions. What is required of now, and the most important exercise to carry forward is a constant and continuous support of women suffering in different context. There are parallels between racial discrimination and gender discrimination. Race is not simply a biological or genetic classification. It is, a way of interpreting differences between people which creates or reinforces inequalities among them.[2] Racism is one

---

1 Ms. Achumlo Ezung is a teaching Faculty at Nagaland Bible College, Artang, Mokokchung, Nagaland.

2 https://www.worldpulse.com/fr/node/7830, accessed on 4/11/15.

of the burning social issues of human race. It has affected millions of people worldwide, and is one of the deepest social problems in history. The term 'racism' is often used in a loose and unreflective way to describe the hostile or negative feelings of one ethnic group or people toward another and the actions resulting from such attitudes[3] often leads to violence, prejudice, oppression, stereotyping, social isolation, bigotry, institutionalizing of beliefs, values and actions etc.[4] This worldwide issue has caused countless problems, particularly among women. So it is imperative that we analyze it for better understanding. When one becomes victim of such behaviour they are terribly devastated and develop a feeling of fear and hatred. Stories of Gender or racial discrimination are often told in the form of rape, torturing and beating, molestation, harassment, etc. Today it's a shame to see how people discriminate against women. Women are sexually harassed, assault termed as 'sluts,' etc., and that proves that there is something terribly wrong in our society. They feel so helpless that they cannot keep on fighting their rights. Each day is a new day, but each day they wonder why they are made to feel discriminated. This is something which I am sure many of us would like to discuss and try to understand the heart and the core of the situation before it gets too late. Therefore, looking into these entire contexts the writer, in this paper will re-imagine gender and racism through prophetic communication.

1. Role of Patriarchy

Here, the writer is referring to the patriarchal structure because the writer felt that it is also one of the roots causes of all the related discrimination that women are facing today. Patriarchy has been a part of our history and its vestiges continue to live in the present times as well. The word "Patriarchy" is derived from two Greek words – Pater meaning 'Father' and Arche meaning 'beginning' or 'first.' It literally means the rule of the father or the patriarch, and originally it was used to describe a specific type of male dominated family- the large household of the patriarch which included women, children, slaves

3 George M. Fredrickson, *Racism: A Short History* (New Jersey: Princeton University Press, 2002), 2.

4 Dean Chavers, *Racism in India Country* (New York: Peter Lang, 2009), 2.

and domestic servants all under the rule of this dominant male.[5] In the social sphere whether it's in cities or rural areas, there are clear evidences of patriarchal dominance. Man is considered superior in articulation, and so they engage in public oratory.[6] Whereas, women were treated as secondary citizens, they have status neither in their parent's homes nor in society. The social system controls women in such a way that she has no other choice except to submit herself to patriarchal values.[7] They are fixed in the homocentric premises of anthropology which creates a distinction between men as we/us and women as they/them.[8] Woman becomes a site that fulfils male sight and desire[9] and compared to luring and vicious serpents and ruthlessly blamed women for tempting men into sin.[10] Women are systematically exploited and became the source through which society exploits, whether through economic or social exploitation.[11]

Narrowing down with regard to Naga society the cultural heritage manifest a multiplicity of women images where women have been alternatively viewed as impure, destructive, opponents and witch. These female images have perceptibly influence towards women to a large extend. Most significantly these images leave a deep imprint upon women self-deception.[12] Women are often

---

5 Kamla Bhasin, *What is Patriarchy?* (New Delhi: Vision Wordtronic Pvt. Ltd., 1993), 3.

6 Michalle Zimbalist Rosaldo, *Women, Culture and Society: A Theoretical Overview, in Women, Culture and Society*, edited by Rosaldo, Michelle Zimbalist and Louise, Lamphere (California: Standard University Press, 1975), 17-19.

7 Metti Amirtham, *Women in India: Negotiating Body, Reclaiming Agency* (Delhi: ISPCK, 2011), 9.

8 Johannes Fabian, *Time and the Other: How Anthropology Makes Its Object* (New York: Columbia University Press, 1983).

9 Sue-Ellen case, *Feminist and Theatre* (London: Macmillan, 1988), 120.

10 Ruth A. Tucker and Walter Liefield, *Daughter of the Church* (Grand Rapids: Zondervan Publishing House, 1987), 131.

11 Ranjani Rebera, *Challenge Patriarchy: Feminist Theology from the Third World,* edited by Ursula King (---: SPCK, 1996), 106-107.

12 Pratiba Jain and Rajan Mahan, (1960), from L. Imsutoshi Jamir and C. Alitemjen Longkumer, *Communication and Naga Culture* (Dimapur: Tribal Development and Communication Centre, 2007), 79.

forced to deny their identity.[13] Some of the Naga folk lore is given in the footnotes where the women were projected as jealous minded, unkind, rude, inhuman treatment towards their step-children etc.[14] In fact, there are many such stories which portray women in a very negative way and distort her image in the society. Therefore, with that patriarchal concept the society still looks at the women with that mentality wherein women become the victim of all the social norms. Every year on March 8th many countries around the world celebrate 'International Women's Day' which was started by Clara Zetkin,[15]

13 Lavina Byrne, *Women Before God* (London; ISPCK, 1988), 7.

14 **Story-1** once upon a time there lived a newly married couple who had a neighbour. Every day as they looked at their neighbour they saw that they neighbours were very happy and the wife were jealous of them. One day she told her husband to make them quarrel among themselves. So the man took his neighbour and told him that they will drink and then beat their own wives. As planned they drank heavily and went back to their respective house and the man pretended to beat his wife and slammed against the blanket and the women started yelling and crying and asked him not to beat her. The neighbour thought that the man is indeed beating his wife and therefore he also started thrashing his own wife without any reason. From that day onwards they were never happy. The jealous woman was finally satisfied because from that time onward she never saw them happy again.

Story-2 There lived a man with two children. The mother died and the man felt that his children need motherly love and therefore married another wife. But unfortunately the women hate the children and ask her husband to leave the children in the field. Therefore, the man sends his children to the field. Every day, the father killed animals and sent the meat to the children through the stepmother but it so happen that the wife never fed them with meat and rice but she used to eat and throw away the remaining and replaced it with stones and some sore fruits. After few years, the father decided to visit his children and when he reached the field and called out to them, they respond from above. The father look up and saw two monkeys and was surprise but they respond that they are his children and never used to eat good food but had survive all these years by eating fruits from the trees because they could not eat what their stepmother gave them. They showed him the food that the stepmother gave them which they collected in a nearby pit. The father was so sad and angry with his wife that he went back and chases her away. (The above Naga folk lore has been passed from generation to generation through oral tradition. It has also been passed down to the writer by her father).

15 Clara Zetkin (5 July 1857-20 June 1933) was a German Marxist theorist, activist, and advocate for women's rights. In 1911, she organized the

an activist for women rights.[16] But regardless of the Women's Day celebration the point I wanted all of us to ponder here is, then why there are lots of discrimination? Why most of the racial victims are women? What is the women status in India? If they are not safe in their own country, where will the safe place be? Are there any solutions for all these questions? Keeping in mind all these query let us look at the present context of racism.

2. Present Scenario of Racism

Today, even though the Indian government gives certain opportunities to the women on the other hand women are facing several issues of racial discrimination, harassment and violence. Discrimination towards women in India is nothing new to report about. There have been instances in the past and present. Cases of sexual harassment, molestation, violence, negative portrayal in media, rape and even deadly attacks, are consistent and relentless. Girls in western outfits are considered loose and seducing. Time and again, various groups of women have experienced forms of racial discrimination and highlighted the practice of racism in India. Following are some of the areas where women are victimized.

Sexual Harassment

Sexual harassment is all about expression of male power over women that sustain patriarchal relations. It is used to remind women of their vulnerability and subjugated status. It is a human rights violation and gender based systemic discrimination that affects women's Right to Life and Livelihood. Sexual harassment can have a devastating effect upon the health, confidence, morale and performance of those affected by it. The question here is why most of the women remain silent about sexual harassment? An absence of complaints about sexual harassment does not necessarily mean an absence of sexual harassment. It may mean that the recipients of sexual harassment think that there is no point in complaining because: nothing will be

first International Women's Day, https://en.wikipedia.org/wiki/Clara_Zetkin, accessed on 30/10/15.

16 Christina Manohar, ed., *Women's Issues and Reflections* (Delhi: ISPCK, 2012), 183.

done about it; it will be trivialised; the complainant will be subjected to ridicule, or they fear retaliation. The best way to prevent sexual harassment is to adopt a comprehensive sexual harassment policy. The aim is to ensure that sexual harassment does not occur and, where it does occur, to ensure that adequate procedures are readily available to deal with the problem and prevent its recurrence.[17]

Sexual Violence

According to the section 375 of Indian Penal Code, Rape can be described as the unlawful intercourse done by a man with a helpless woman. Due to such kind of activities, a woman lives a pathetic life which causes fear, depression, guilt complex, suicidal action and other kind of social stigma that humiliates women for their entire life.

Effects of Rape: a) **3 times** more likely to suffer from depression. b) **6 times** more likely to suffer from post-traumatic stress disorder. c) **13 times** more likely to abuse alcohol. d) **26 times** more likely to abuse drugs. e) **4 times** more likely to contemplate suicide.

Negative Portrayal of Women in Media

In recent years it has been observed that the media has emerged in a big way as the major exploiter of woman, with changing times new ways of expression social power have been fashioned which target the weaker components of society. The most vulnerable target is women.

Women play a very significant role in advertising today both as consumer and as influencers. The depiction of women in Indian advertising has been a topic of debate for a while now. The experts against the indecent representation of women in advertising strongly believe that the women's moral and social status is mainly determined on the basis of the degree of exposure of her physical form to public view. Women advertising redefine women attractiveness as something that is away from natural. There are advertisements where the females are shown in bad light. They are clad in skimpy clothes even when their presence in the advertisements has no relevance with

17 *THE NEWS IN PROPORTION*, (4 November 2015), http://indiatogether.org/combatlaw/vol2/issue3/harass.htm, accessed on 4/11/15.

the brand. In the exchange between the 'commodity' and 'woman' in advertisements, a woman becomes a commodity, too. Women are portrayed as sex objects who are probably cast to titillate the viewers by exposing their body parts. Women are used as models exposing their bodies. Glamour dolls in front of the cameras and ace photographers do the same behind the lenses thus trapping thousands of teenagers to believe in the miracle of the product.

Gender Discrimination in Indian Churches

How is women's status in India churches? Today's India offers a lot of opportunities to women, with women having a voice in everyday life, the business world as well as in political life. Nevertheless, India is still a male dominated society, where women are often seen as subordinate and inferior to men. The status of woman in the Church is no exception to the reality of society around. As a matter of fact, in reality, the Church has been covering far behind the secular movements and achievements in redressing gender inequalities. The role of women in the Church works is biased. Even during Jesus' time, women were active as active as men but most women's activeness was not recorded. The Church has managed to silence women over the centuries and promote them secondary position in the name of Scripture, Church tradition and socio-cultural context. Whenever, women have protested against the discrimination faced by them in church and society. The Bible has been referred to, to indicate that the secondary status of women is divinely ordained - woman was made after man, she brought sin and death into the world, Christ had no woman disciples; Paul has called on women to be silent in the church and to be obedient to their husbands (1 Cor 14: 34). These are some of the more commonly used arguments to support such a stand. Women are urged therefore, to be submissive wives and live according to the biblical 'teachings' on womanhood.[18] The Church has bestowed a greater authority on the Scriptures to express its Faiths, Tradition and Practice. The Scriptures are considered to be one of the main sources for doing theology. The manners in which they read, understand and interpret thus pave the way for different types of theological education that reinforce patriarchy. Within

18 http://www.youtube.com/watch?v=SZY4v_nnIKA, accessed on 4/11/15.

this framework women too have largely been influenced and have never really had the courage to challenge the discrimination they face. Their religious education and the teachings of the church have socialized Christian women to accept this so-called God-ordained discrimination. Today patriarchy is one of the challenges for Indian churches.[19]

3. Responses through Prophetic Communication

The fact that God chooses to communicate through history means that God uses human culture as the vehicle of communication with humankind. The use of human messengers to speak to the human frame of reference reveals God as continually seeking out humankind to enter into a covenantal relationship. For Christians the events or the day are parts of God agenda for action. In it, God's plans are revealed through the changing circumstances and new opportunities. In order to discern and interpret the situation correctly, Christian communicators must listen to God and be led by the spirit. This is a condition or prophecy.[20]

The rise of racism should not be a surprise to Christians who are watching for the return of Jesus Christ. We know that society will not get better prior to the Lord's return, the apostle Paul said it would get worse in 2 Timothy 3:1-5,13.[21] Jesus Christ cited racial strife as one of the signs of His soon return in Luke 21:10. *Nation will rise against nation and kingdom against kingdom.* The Greek word from the original text translated 'nation' is 'ethnos' which means a people or race. It is evident that our world is in turmoil and in need of great

19 http://www.opportunity.org/?utm_campaign=381&utm_term, accessed on 4/11/15.

20 L. Imsutoshi Jamir, *A Basic Guide to Communication Studies* (Jorhat: TDCC, 2010), 133.

21 Vs. 1 you must understand this, that in the last days distressing times will come. 2 For people will be lovers of themselves, lovers of money, boasters, arrogant, abusive, disobedient to their parents, ungrateful, unhly, 3 inhuman, implacable, slanders, profligates, brutes, haters of good, 4 treacherous, reckless, swollen with conceit, lovers of pleasure rather than God, 5 holding to the outward form of godliness but denying its power. Avoid them! Vs. 13 but wicked people and impostors will go from bad to worse, deceiving others and being deceived. (NRSV)

nurturing. Robert Wicks, in his book, *Touching the Holy* tells us that ... the call from God to nurture others as we nurture ourselves... this can lead to true compassion, sound friendship, and effective social action.[22] Jesus reminded the Pharisees of the great commandment, *you shall love your neighbour as yourself* in Matthew 22:39. The Pharisees being the legalists they were responded by asking, *and who is my neighbour?* (Luke 10:29). Christ answered this with the parable of the Good Samaritan who helped a Jew who had been mugged. The Samaritan helped the Jew despite the hatred between the two races (Luke 10:30-37). This teaches that everyone is our neighbour and we should even love those who hate us (Matthew 5:44).

The Bible shows that neither the man nor the woman has a special advantage in being a Christian. Christ does not choose men in preference to women, or relate to men more directly. It is true that women are dependent upon men, yet it is equally true that men are dependent upon women. *Neither is the man without the woman, neither the woman without the man, in the Lord* (1 Corinthians 11:11). They are *heirs together to the grace of life* (1 Peter 3:7). *God created humankind in His own image...male and female* (Genesis 1:27, 5:1-2). Both of them together are the likeness of God.

Racism, in varying forms and to various degrees, has been a plague on humanity for thousands of years. Brothers and sisters of all ethnicities, this should not be. Victims of racism, prejudice, and discrimination need to forgive. Ephesians 4:32 declares, *be kind and compassionate to one another, forgiving each other, just as in Christ God forgave you.* Racists may not deserve your forgiveness, but we deserved God's forgiveness far less. Those who are practicing racism, prejudice, and discrimination need to repent. *Present yourselves to God as being alive from the dead, and your members as instruments of righteousness to God* (Romans 6:13). Galatians 3:28 is the completely realized, *There is neither Jew nor Greek, slave nor free, male nor female, for you are all one in Christ Jesus.* Paul also taught that, *There is no partiality with God* (Romans 2:11, Ephesians 6:9)[23] James said that

22 Robert J. Wicks, *Touching the Holy* (Notre Dame: Ave Press, 1992), 9.

23 Vs. 9 "And, masters, do the same to them, stop threatening them, for you know that both of you have the same master in heaven, and with them there is no partiality." (NRSV).

having prejudices about people different from us was sin (James 2:1-9). When we have prejudices, we are judging others which are sin, *for in whatever you judge another you condemn yourself; for you who judge practice the same things* (Romans 2:1; see also James 4:11-12).

God Himself elevated the status of women forever when He chose to send His own Son, Jesus Christ, to be born of a virgin. The words and actions of Jesus underscored His elevated opinion of women. His first miracle was performed in response to a plea from His mother (John 2:1-11), His first revelation of Himself as Messiah was to a woman (John 4:25-26), His death was memorialized by a woman (John 12:1-8), Women were included in His expanded group of disciples (Mark 15:41), Women stayed with Him throughout His crucifixion, even after the men had left (Matthew 27:55-56), Women observed His burial (Matthew 27:61), Following His resurrection, He appeared first to a woman (John 20:1-16), He commissioned women as the very first evangelists (Matthew 28:1-10; John 20:17), Women were included in the group of disciples who met daily for prayer after the ascension of Jesus (Acts 1:14), Ancient prophecy was fulfilled when the Spirit of God was given equally to men and women at Pentecost (Acts 2:17), Women were among the very first "believers" or "Christians" who made up the early church (Acts 5:14; Acts 8:12; 17:4, 12).

The very fact that the Bible goes out of its way to carefully record all of the above reveals the intentionality of God's purpose to reestablish the position of women to that of equality with men. His Son, Jesus Christ, not only bridged the gap between God and man through His death on the Cross that made atonement for man's sin, He removed all barriers including that of gender, race, and nationality. Paul taught the gospel to both Jews and Gentiles, *for it is the power of God to salvation for everyone who believes* (Romans 1:16).

If we are true followers of Christ, we will obey his command to, *make disciples of all the nations* regardless of race (Matthew 28:19). All races will be represented in heaven, *out of every tribe and tongue and people and nation* (Revelation 5:9). The Bible tells us that all men were created in the image of God (Genesis 1:26). *Have we not all one Father? Has not one God created us? Why then are we faithless to one another profaning the covenant of our ancestors?* (Malachi 2:10).[24] Michael J. Cunningham, in his book states, "the mystic tell us that we don't have to find God outside ourselves, but to awaken to the pearl of great price, which is already given to us."[25]

This is an important time for all Christians to lead in positive extremes of a bright future tackling evil with love and with intentional efforts to bring unity that is so desperately needed. There is no greater witness for Christ, no greater stand for truth and unity than to speak up and speak out.

This is a call for all Christians to condemn the lingering negative attitudes on the basis of race and hate in every segment of society. Racial evil is not few groups problem but it is a human problem. We can no longer ignore racism. We must confront it, name it, reject it, fight it, kill it, and forbid it. If we are to build a better society for our generation, we must snuff out the evil with a slogan "Let's talk and heal together."

Prophetic communication needs to take into account that there is a need for self examination and accountability even of the Church itself. Perhaps, that is where the beginning should be. Indeed, the church is called to proclaim God's judgments on all that opposes God's way of justice and fullness of life; but it also requires judgment for its own participation in the conditions that create brokenness. Silence of the Church in the face of those screaming for help is nothing other than disobedience to God and to the prophetic call of the Christian community. The prophetic call of communication should be understood from the point of view of content rather than structures; people rather than technology; justice rather than ability. The prophetic action of Christian communities lies in its efforts to sustain life and bring justice to God's world. Christian communication is also called to challenge the power structures in communication in order to find a breakthrough, which will give voice to the powerless. The church is to be a prophetic community characterized among other things by its struggle for inclusiveness,

---

24 Scott Huckaby, *The Biblical Response to Racism*, http://www.bibletract.org/essays/racism.htm, accessed on 1/11/15.

25 Michael J. Cunningham, *Treasure Within Rediscovering the Mystic* (Bolton: Don Bosco Publications, 2011), 88.

trust, responsibility, justice and love. A church cannot be prophetic unless it constantly fights inherent tendencies towards exclusiveness. Inclusive communication makes everyone an active part of the communicative event.

But words are only part of prophesy. They take on real meaning only when they are accompanied by action. Prophetic communication expresses itself in words and deeds. Such prophetic action must be willing to challenge the principalities and powers, and many carry a high price. Prophetic communication serves truth and challenges falsehood. Lies and half-truths are a great threat to communication. Prophetic communication stimulates critical awareness of the reality constructed by the society and help to distinguish truth from falsehood.[26]

4. Some Suggestions

We need progressive voices today, in every culture and community, to proclaim loudly the concerns of women and to affirm life and full humanity for all.[27] Women need to define themselves but, in order to do that, they need autonomy and their own space to break down various definitions that see them as other in order to create their own definition of themselves, in which they are central.[28] We need new ways of engagement. The Christian community must lift up our voices like a trumpet. Why should we be silent on issues that matter to common humanity? Racism is evil. I want to borrow from Dr. Martin Luther King's eulogy "to transform the negative extremes of a dark past into the positive extremes of a bright future."

Here are some of the constitutional provisions that give protection for women. Women should know their rights. Empowerment of women is one of the nine primary objectives of India's IX Plan (1997-2002) and every effort is being made to create an enabling environment where women can freely exercise their rights within and outside their home, as equal partners with man.

---

26 L. Imsutoshi Jamir, *A Basic Guide to Communication Studies..*, 134.

27 Michelene Wandor, *Voices are Wild, in Women's Writing: A Challenge to Theory*, 72-82.

28 Gerda Lerner, *The Creation of Feminist Consciousness* (Oxford: Oxford University Press, 1993), 19.

Article 14 of the Indian Constitution ensures equality before law to all persons within the territory of India. The strict compliance with rule is obligatory on the part of the state and a citizen cannot waive this right. Article 15 prohibits discrimination on the basis of sex or religion, race caste, place of birth and any of them. Similarly, under Article 16 no citizen should be subjected to any disability or restriction to hold public offices or Public employment.[29] At the same time the constitution of India, Article 15 (3) provides for affirmative and positive action in favour of women by empowering the state to make special provisions for them. Sexual Harassment is covered under the peculiar title 'Violation of a Women's Modesty' under Indian Panel Code 354.[30]

We can see codified laws protecting women are in plenty but how far it is protection women in reality is a million dollar question which needs to be assessed properly. Women should not just remain ignorant, blind and suppressed but contribute to the upliftment and come to the realization of one's rights.

Somebody said, the world is a dangerous place to live not because of the alien's people but because of the people who don't do anything about it. We should not forget that every citizen contributes his/her share of duties and services for the common welfare of the republic.[31] Keeping in mind the above statements, following are some of the suggestions:

1. Tolerance along with Acceptance will only make a difference. Tolerance has a limit, but acceptance is a decision, and a wise decision must add. Once you have accepted someone with a sound mind and body you can never regret it even if you want to. That's what we need. Plus, right from the elementary school children must be taught of equality.

---

29 Nirmala Jeyaraj, ed., *Women and Society: A Reader in Women's Studies* (Delhi: ISPCK, 2008), 365.

30 Northeast Herald, 9 June, 2001.

31 Tajen Ao, *Ao Naga Customary Law* (Mokokchung: Tribal Gospel Publisher Shoppe, 1980), 14.

2. To eliminate racism against women, the platform for action should be set up to condemn racism and enforce and enact legislation against perpetrators of practices and act of violence against women.
3. The need for unity, unity here is not political unity or social unity but the unity of the whole womanhood in the world. The unity of the women can help very much to reduce their hardships. Every nation has its own problems. Yet the women's forum will accelerate welfare measure among women in the respective countries.[32]
4. Listen to one another: Joan Chittister says in her book, *The Fire in These Ashes...*, "we all need to listen to every other word around it, it deserves to be heard as well or the total truth may never be known."[33]
5. The solution to racism also requires commitment and participation by every individual regardless of their cultural origin.
6. Although, there is no perfect way to solve racism problem. What we can do however is to limit its extent as much as possible. I think that the best way to solve this problem is knowledge.
7. Willingness among the leadership to change the oppressive structures and create new and liberative act.
8. It is important to re-read the Bible to re-discover the hidden works and the achievements of women.
9. Strengthen Christian education and family education programmers of the church to develop positive attitudes towards women, especially to ensure security for the girl child in the Indian Homes.[34]

---

32 K. A. Kunjakkan, *Feminism and Indian Realities* (New Delhi: Mittal Publications, 2002), 402-403.

33 Joan Chittister, *The Fire in these Ashes* (Kansas: Sheed & Ward, 1995), 134.

34 Kumari Prasanna, *Feminist Thelogy Perspectives and Praxis* (Gurukul Summer Institute Chennai, 1998).

Conclusion

Gendered Racism has long been ignored, suffered through, and dealt with by many people. In addition, there are still many people who object to bringing up the subject. Racism and discrimination should be exposed and dealt with. Men and women, working together, will lead towards the revaluing and reconstructing of their relationships at home and society. A peaceful home and a peaceful society should be our goal. Aung San Suu Kyi[35] said in her Nobel Peace Prize speech on 16th June 2012:

> Absolute peace in our world is an unattainable goal. But it is one towards which we must continue to journey, our eyes fixed on it a travellers in a desert fixes his eyes on the one guiding star that will lead him to salvation. Even if we do not achieve perfect peace on earth, because perfect peace is not of this earth, common endeavours to gain peace will unite individuals and nations in trust and friendship and help to make our human community safer and kinder.[36]

Silence is no longer an option, we need to talk speak out, more debates and awareness has to be created. The reason for fighting against racism is not because it is practised against our own citizens but because it is wrong regardless of whether the victims of racism are citizens of the country or not. One way to be critical of racism is to recognise and make visible the presence of racism rather than merely resorting to legalistic means to curb this discrimination. Every person has the same position in the world, we couldn't look down to anyone.

Here, attempt has been made to explore re-imagining of gender and racism through prophetic communication with the hope to find out some solution. Only a few aspects of the solution from the clutches of racism could be explored, much more remains to be investigated. Yet, in the few aspects that we explored, it is discovered that several elements of solution have meted out, which can be use to

---

35 Aung San Suu Kyi born on 19 June 1945 is a Burmese opposition political and chairperson of the National League for Democracy (NLD) in Burma, https://en.wikipedia.org/wiki/Aung_San_Suu_Kyi, accessed on 28/10/15.

36 Christina Manohar, ed., *Women's Issues and Reflections..*, 201.

give new expression and recognition to the women. This should form the basis to live peacefully and give equal opportunities and privileges to all women without any discrimination in every aspect of life. It is discovered that through the years, racism is increasing in many areas. The only issue was that it has never been re-imagined. Therefore, it is the hope of this writer that this will serve as an incentive for further investigation to give new expression to the racism and that equality is being done to all the humanity.

12

Racism and Christian Ministry Call to Witness as an Inclusive Church for a Just and Humane Community

Imtimenba Jamir[1]

The central theme of the seminar *Racism: The Thorn in Humanity's Coexistence* is a call to reflection and action in a violent and culturally fragmented world, that threatens to tear apart the social fabric of our existence and the emotional ties that binds us together. This trend is a serious concern that needs our attention as citizens of India and as a faith community. I am grateful to Clark Centre for Peace Research and Action for giving me this privilege to be a part of this important initiative.

The theme has been thoroughly examined from the perspectives of Sociology, The Bible, Theology, History, Communication, Law, and Ethics. In the course of our discussion plenty of illustrations have already been highlighted, and there is a healthy eagerness to explore the terrain toward building an inclusive community of believers and to be true witnesses to the world.

The main concern in this paper is how do we negate negativity and move towards an inclusive Church. My focus is predominantly limited to the role of Churches in dealing with racial discrimination face by Northeast people in the metro cities in India.

---

1 Mr. Imtimenba Jamir is the Assistant Director at the Centre for Dalit/Subaltern Studies, New Delhi.

1. Racial Prejudices North East People face in the Metropolitan Cities in India

All citizens of India have the right to go to any part of the country; many young people from the north-eastern states go to places of their choice for studies and huge sections of young people migrate to different places for employment outside the north-eastern states. Such trend facilitates a closer contact, interaction and intermingling between the people and expose them to different racial background, culture, practices, costumes, food habits, prejudices, etc.

The consequences of such exposure is beyond the scope of this paper, yet most notably in the recent past, there have been a steady raise of violence and discriminatory practices being reported and witnessed against the people from the north-eastern states in different parts of India. They are being targeted in diverse ways: either harassed or sexually molested or beaten up or ridiculed or in some cases killed. The physical attacks and verbal abuse such as making derogatory names and remarks are on the rise conspicuously in almost all metropolitan cities in India.

For most of the north-easterners everyday living in Indian cities can be a gruelling experience. Be it the mundane overcharging of fares by autoricksaw-*wallahs*, shopkeepers and landlords, the verbal abuse on the streets and the snide remarks bycolleagues, friends, teachers, if a teacher by students or the more extreme experiences of physical and sexual assaults. It is often a never-ending chronicle of repetitive experience just because of "the particular looks" of north-easterners.

Such actions and utterances on one hand generally portray the 'depth of ignorance' among the masses of Indian populace. Knowledge about diversity of Indian people, race, culture, practices, costumes and habits are very shallow not only amongst the general public but surprisingly even among the so-called 'educated people.' On the other hand, due to the racial appearance in the form of different looks, language, cultural barriers and alien-sounding, difficult-to-pronounce names north-easterners are viewed as outsiders and beyond the Indian social fabric. This xenophobia leads to hostility and alienation as they don't fit in Indian standard norms and societal framework. Such ignorance combined with cultural arrogance and insensitivity are often the breeding grounds for many racially related incidents.

In general three broader forms of racism are face by the north-easterners in the cities in India. The recent murder of a 19 years old tribal young man Nido Tania on 30th January 2015 in Delhi, from the state of Arunachal Pradesh[2] was perpetrated by miscreants when Nido reacted to mockery for his longish, stylized, dyed hair, and clothing and physical features. This incident is just an instance of deeply emboldened hostile attitude of the locals against these foreign-looking people. A tragic reminder that violence has taken roots between people who share the same territory but differ in ethnicity, race, language or religion.

In a case of 'institutional racism,' the University of Hyderabad launched an "initiative" in 2011 to curb drinking and drug use on campus by working with students from the north-east, a clear case of racism racial profiling.[3] In 2007, the Delhi Police decided to solve the problems of security faced by the north-easterners in Delhi, particularly women, by coming up with a booklet entitled *Security Tips for North East Students* asking north-eastern women not to wear "revealing dresses" and gave kitchen tips on preparing bamboo shoot, *akhuni*, and "other smelly dishes" without "creating ruckus in neighbourhood."[4]

Moreover, racial prejudices experienced in subtle forms in everyday interactions with random people in the streets, at neighbourhood markets and at different places are more felt than directly experienced, but is no less unsettling. It comes in the form of snide remarks, unwelcome staring, smirks and stereotyping about

---

2 *Arunachal MLA's son 'beaten to death' in Delhi, anger spills over,* in http://timesofindia.indiatimes.com/city/delhi/Arunachal-MLAs-son-beaten-to-death-in-Delhi-anger-spills-over/articleshow/29672979.cms accessed on 12 October 2015.

3 *'Racial profiling' in Hyderabad University sparks row by Nikhila Henry & Mahesh Buddi,* in http://timesofindia.indiatimes.com/india/Racial-profiling-in-Hyderabad-university-sparks-row/articleshow/10457371.cms, accessed on 20 October 2015.

4 *"Be safe, don't exist" by Kalpana Sharma* in http://www.thehindu.com/todays-paper/tp-features/tp-sundaymagazine/article2275456.ece, accessed on 20 October 2015.

clothing and sexuality. It is difficult to prove such kind of racism, it is most often felt, perceived, like an invisible wound, difficult to articulate or recall in the language of the law or evidence. Such experiential rather than objectively identifiable situations are the most common racial discrimination Northeast people faces almost on daily basis in the metropolitan cities in India.

2. The Otherness Demands our Attention

Today there is a shift in interest from universal to particular, from global to local, from equality to difference. This shift is constructed on the understanding that "universality" is available only from within a given "particularity." In this context the narratives of identity emphasises recognition - unique identity, distinctiveness which cannot be ignored nor assimilated to a dominant or majority identity. In this sense the racial conflicts or discriminations which we witness are part of a larger problem of identity and otherness.

The fact that most of the Northeastern communities while living outside our states do form small groups and churches on the line of their respective tribes and state. As minorities there is a strong feeling of congregating together for social security, to help each other in times of needs, hardship, sickness, death, to satisfy our social and religious needs, and most importantly to preserve ones culture and identity. Such community based congregations becomes a necessity and the only social security for most of the Northeast people living in different cities of India. And on many cases these organizations are the only available platforms to comfort each together as well as to take-up cases of mistreatments and other situations collectively. But when we talk about OUR rights, OUR identity and OUR equality we need to remember that stress on equality makes sense only as a way of addressing the concerns of differences or the otherness. We may say that we welcome anyone into our groups, fellowships, churches, etc. But as a matter of fact there is always a thick wall demarcating the group, almost impossible to penetrate unless one has all the requisite criterions to be a member or part of that group. Such very nature of our congregating together as smaller people groups sends out the message that "others" are not at all welcome! And communal segregation is largely a result of racism.

This is not to say that it is wrong to have such community based congregations. There is nothing wrong to assert and fight for OUR rights. But when we do that, are we also giving away the same rights to others? We cannot simply claim that our ways are better and therefore others must accept us as we are. It is also their right not to accept us if they decide to do so. There is a down side of this if we, on one hand, fight for OUR rights and justice but on the other hand have feeling of resentment against those who have violated our rights. If this is true, we have never been really fighting for justice; we were simply fighting for our rights but not for equal rights. True justice on equality is delivered only when "everyone," including the one who have violated your rights, have equal rights. We are selfish beings living among selfish fellow human. There is a fatal disease called "me." This disease makes us demand justice when we have ourselves failed to deliver justice to others.

It is true that many people living in other parts of India have the wrong information about people from the Northeast. While a big part of this information is provided by the media, books, etc., and first hand information by those who have visited the Northeast. However, a rather large part of this information is contributed by our own people living in other parts of India. The question is how we are projecting ourselves to the 'others'? As individuals we bear the responsibility to be ambassadors of our respective social identities to the others who are less knowledgeable about the people, customs, practices, habits, etc of Northeast India.

It will be appropriate to mention three popular ways adopted to address the problem of otherness:

Firstly, there are laws to protect people from discrimination and deprivations based on race, gender, caste and religion. Law is one of the most effective ways to bring wrongdoers to justice and be punished, but this will not prevent racism at the core. This may perhaps check institutional racism but it will only identify racial attacks and deal with it at the judicial level. It will not really take away negative racial attitudes.

Secondly, there is a proposal to educate the people of mainland India and bringing awareness to them about the Northeastern states by including its history in the text books[5] including proposals to organize festivals and establish museums and information centers to create awareness about the region.[6] Proposals to these initiatives will no doubt provide a large amount of information about the Northeast but cannot totally eradicate the problem of racism.

Thirdly, yet another way to approach the problem is the proposal to have more people from the North East to represent in different government workforce such as the recruitment of NE youth into the Delhi Police.[7] The general view is that the presence of North East people in different fields will give them less alienated and help people from the region in times of need.

These initiatives definitely are potential apparatus to help people who are being mistreated as well as to challenge this problem. However, they are limited to as much as the constitutional judiciary system has to offer. It may ease the problem to some extent but racism will still exist. The question we must ask is, is there another way? It will be appropriate here to discuss the role of the Church and Christians to the problem of racism North East people face in India.

3. Christian Witness in Society

It is generally understood that Christian witness is to lead the people to the saving knowledge of Lord Christ who died for the sins of humanity. More often Christian witness has been limited only to

5 *CBSE to create better awareness on northeast states*, in http://indiatoday.intoday.in/education/story/cbse-to-create-better-awareness-on-northeast-states/1/414563.html, *Soon, northeast history, culture in textbooks* In http://www.thehindu.com/todays-paper/tp-in-school/soon-northeast-history-culture-in-textbooks/article5710946.ece, accessed on 20 October 2015.

6 *Northeast festival to raise awareness in Delhi*, in http://www.newswala.com/India-National-News/northeast-festival-to-raise-awareness-in-delhi-101755.html; *Discover North East programme to create awareness about India's northeast region held at Guwahati*, in http://www.newswala.com/India-National-News/discover-north-east-to-create-awareness-about-region-98361.html, accessed on 20 October 2015.

7 *411 NE youth to join Delhi Police*, in http://www.nagalandpost.com/ChannelNews/National/NationalNews.aspx?news=TkVXUzEwMDA5MjU0Mw%3D%3D, accessed on 23 January 2016.

the activity of soul saving. This kind of interpretation has rendered many Churches and Christians insensitive to the issues within and outside the Church. Undoubtedly Northeast churches and Christian fellowships in the metro cities particularly in Delhi fall within this category. Usually in any kind of incidents or racial discrimination/ violence the Pastors, Chaplains or Church workers from Northeast are amongst the first to respond and help the victims. But collective as a Church very little has been done by any Northeastern churches in Delhi to address the issue of racial discrimination that northeast people face in Delhi.

I believe the Churches and Christian fellowships must have more pressing concerns and issues to deal with or they might be considering racial discrimination or racism northeast people face in metro cities like Delhi as something beyond the realm of Christian witness, an issue that fall within the domain of the state, the law or the civil society. According to Philipose Mar Chrysostom "Evangelism is God going out to the world, loving the world, taking form in the world, living in the world dying for the world and returning in glory to consummate the world."[8] It means the world is the locus of Christian witness. This world includes people under different forms of victimization, people subjected to varied forms of exploitation, etc. Therefore, Christian witness cannot be complete unless and until it touches the issues of the people in the society. This is the standpoint of Gospel of Jesus Christ. M.M. Thomas said, "Humanization is inherent in the message of salvation in Christ"[9]

A genuine Christian witness responds to the realities of human life. It defends the rights of victims and fights for the people at the margins. It stands for the liberation of people as Jesus did in His earthly ministry. According to Samuel Amirtham, "Jesus' proclamation of the Good news is evangelization, which means that those who are in various kinds of bondage, in prisons of poverty and powerlessness, under the bonds of ignorance and superstitions

8 Metropolitan Philipose Mar Chrysostom, "Mission in the Market Place," in *World Evangelism and Christian Leadership,* edited by J.T.K. Daniel (Delhi: ISPCK, 2005), 246.

9 M.M. Thomas, *Salvation and Humanization* (Madras: The CLS, 1971), 10.

and the victims of oppression and injustices are free."[10] It indicates that building a just and humane community is the goal of Christian witness in this world. It naturally includes all types of interventions to affirm life against victimization, discrimination and oppression. A just and humane community refers to a community/social life where people experience life-affirmation over life-negation.

In such a context, Christian theologies and ministries, are enterprises that involves flesh-and-blood people in a given context; it is a creative witness, reflecting the creative activity of the Holy Spirit, who is the Spirit of life and movement in a world in which God is continuously and intimately involved. God lives and moves amongst his people, whose story is not a story in isolation, but one that interacts with every human story. We are all participants in God's story, as we are Christ's witness on earth.

This is not to argue for a model of ministry that permits the context to set the agenda for the Christian church: the gospel is a proactive and transformative presence in the world. So the challenge is to engage with the world in such a way as to retain both cultural relevance and gospel-faithfulness, without falling into either cultural naivety or dogmatic fundamentalism.

Therefore, the core purpose of the Christian faith-community is a commitment to ensuring freedom for all and sets the example in condemning injustice. God himself deplores the injustices of individuals and society. God wills Justice, peace, harmony and righteousness as it goes hand in hand.

4. Witnessing within the Christian Community- a model for Just and Humane Community

The space of Christian witness is not only outside the Church but also inside the church. It should start first within the community, and then move out to the world. In the words of Gustavo Gutierrez, "To be a Christian is to accept and to live-in solidarity, in faith, hope and charity."[11] It implies that the Christian community should

10 Israel Selvanayagam, *Samuel Amirtham's Living Theology* (Bangalore: BTESSC\ SATHRI, 2007), 442.

11 Gustavo Gutierrez, *A Theology of Liberation* (New York: Orbis Books, 1973), 49.

become the presence of Jesus Christ, who denounced discrimination and attempted to establish a just and humane community on earth. It should become a community of denouncing life-negating forces/ practices and of practicing Jesus' Good news of love, justice and peace. Witnessing within the community refers to combating against evils of race, gender prejudices, corruption, caste, denominational mentality pro-rich attitude, etc. In other words beyond all these barriers the Christian community in respective context should become a humane community where kingdom values are the criteria for community building/life.

Without addressing to the problems/issues within the community, Christian witness will not be fruitful in the larger society. As part of witnessing, churches of different traditions should convergence on common agenda to make Christian community a model for justice and humane community. It will help the Christians to have collective thinking and action beyond narrow denominational barriers to bring the Reign of earth.

5. Witness as Affirmation of all Cultures and Rejection of Exclusion

At the very core of Christian identity lies an all-encompassing change of loyalty, from a given culture with its gods to the God of all cultures. There is a reality that is more important than the culture to which we belong. It is God and the new world that God is creating, a world in which people from every nation and every tribe, with and their cultural goods, will gather around the triune God, a world in which every tear will be wiped away and "pain will be no more" (Revelation 21:3).

The allegiance to God creates space in us to receive the other. Consider what happens when a person becomes a Christian. Paul writes, "So if anyone is in Christ, there is a new creation" (2 Corinthians 5:17). God brings a whole new world. The Spirit of God breaks through the self-enclosed worlds we inhabit; the Spirit recreates us and sets us on the road toward becoming a new creation, a new personality enriched by otherness.

We must reject exclusion for it entails cutting of the bonds that connect, taking oneself out of the pattern of interdependence and placing oneself in a position of sovereign independence. The other then emerges either as an enemy that must be pushed away from the self and driven out of its space or as a nonentity—a superfluous being—that can be disregarded and abandoned.

Exclusion can entail removal of separation, not recognizing the other as someone who in his or her otherness belongs to the pattern of interdependence. The other then emerges as an inferior being who must either be assimilated by being made like the self or be subjugated to the self.

Exclusion takes place when the violence of expulsion, assimilation, or subjugation and the indifference of abandonment replace the dynamics of taking in and keeping out as well as the mutuality of giving and receiving.

In the battle against evil, especially against the evil in one's own society, the Church needs ecumenical community. In order to keep our allegiance to Jesus Christ pure, we need to nurture commitment to the multicultural community of Christian churches. We need to see ourselves and our own understanding of God's future with the eyes of Christians from other cultures, listen to voices from other cultures so as to make sure that the voice of our culture has not drowned out the voice of Jesus Christ. An important step that would destroys and eliminate the existing walls of exclusion and move towards a community of integration and mutual affirmation would be a 'celebration of pluralism.' A pluralism that imply 'I affirm my identity,' 'I affirm your identity,' leading to a healthy pluralism, a step towards mutual acceptance, respect, and affirmation of the beauty of diversity.

Just as God has embraced us in the person of Christ we are also called to embrace the other and join together, we are called to a life-long commitment—to join this challenging salvation journey and to take proactive responsibility for the process.

We are called to hold together the belief and affirm that all people are created in the image of God with the commitment to overcome the inherent barriers to fully living out that image. While there are many barriers—and while every category of difference brings with it complex histories, dynamics, and challenges for us to understand and explore—we believe that addressing the particular problem of racism and focusing on building a racially inclusive church and society will be the means toward our goal of building a just and humane community a total congregational culture fuelled by grace/inclusion/action/change for all people, in every sphere of life: heart, church, and the society.

6. Converging with Life-affirming Forces a Goal of Witnessing

To contain the abuses committed in the name of race, ethnicity, caste or religious groups remains a foremost challenge for us as Christians. It demands the convergence of all life affirming forces.

To build a just and humane society is possible only through responding to the contemporary human realities irrespective of religio-cultural-ethnic identities/boundaries. It directly points to the active involvement of the Christian community to reclaim justice. Christian witness in India becomes valid if it addresses the vital issues of the society because involvement in human struggles is the prophetic witness of Jesus.[12] To be oblivious of these issues or to deny its existence is to legitimise the discriminatory regime. Also, the reason for fighting against racism is not because it is practised against "our" own people but because it is wrong regardless of whether the victims of racism are citizens of the country or not. One way to be critical of racism is to recognise and make visible the presence of racism rather than merely resorting to legalistic means to curb this discrimination.

To build a just and humane society free of discrimination based on race, ethnicity, caste and religion in a pluralistic context like India is to join hands (convergence) with life-affirming forces such as other religious communities and civil society groups that uphold and affirm life. We should recognise that every religion has elements and values of life-affirmation. That should be tapped and activated through dialogue with different religions along with different sections of the Church that fast-spreading evils of discrimination, violence, and religious fundamentalism can be effectively dealt with

12 Paulose Mar Paulose, *Spirituality for Struggle* (Thiruvalla: CSS, 1999), 28.

by the Church and society.[13] The Christian community cannot be afraid to take up the issues of the people along with other religious communities and movements. What we need today is not a timid Christian community which is hesitant to align with life-affirming forces in the nation.[14]

The North East communities need to go beyond their narrow exclusive tribal based organizations and initiate broader relevant studies, research and programmes on serious issues that their people face today in the Cities. In a city like Delhi they can collaborate with relevant departments of universities like - Delhi University, Jawaharlal Nehru University, Jamia Millia Islamia and others. Appropriate programmes can be initiated with relevant Government agencies and Ministries that are tasked with such concerns. We need to work together to affirm equal rights for all to gain a greater understanding of the underlying causes of racial discrimination and social exclusion. The root causes to these problems can then be attacked through a variety of measures and initiatives.

Almost all North East communities have their respective social organizations and churches in the metropolitan cities. These organizations and churches need to take more pro-active role to help the new comers as they move to a more complex society in the metropolitan cities. They can initiate orientation programmes to help and educate new comers to adopt and smoothly adjust into the new environment, handle the cultural differences, make them aware of the likes and dislikes, and also the dangers, etc.

Every man, woman and child is entitled to enjoy their human rights, on the basis of their humanity and regardless of any distinguishing characteristics - such as race, gender, creed, opinion or class.[15] But we as the 'other' living outside our native environment,

---

13 Catholic Bishops' Conference of India (CBCI), "The Church in Dialogue," Final Statement of 25th General Body Meeting (Jalandhar, March 1-8, 2002) quoted in *Theramma* Prayikalam, *Manakaruth Spirituality of Fisherwomen: Inspiration and Challenge to Consecrated Women*, 61.

14 John Dayal, "Guest Editorial: Setting a Course for the Indian Church," *Vidyajyoti Journal of Theological Reflection*, Vol. 77/no 6 (June: 2013), 1-4 at 3.

15 *Human Rights. A Compilation of International Instruments, Volume I* (First Part), Universal Instruments (New York and Geneva: 1994), 30.

it is our responsibility to understand and learn from the diversity of cultural and tread with respect the cultural sensitivities of the host societies. Above all, every individual person must realize that we are ambassadors of our people, and therefore we must be exemplary witnesses of our people to other communities who are less knowledgeable about out people.

North East communities must work to create opportunities to increase awareness of the connections we all share. To remind of our similarities and celebrate our differences and to allow the positive energy of oneness in diversity to emerge in a world that too often seems disconnected and broken. The rich diversity of India constantly remind us that we are all on a journey to better understand ourselves, our connections with others, and our ultimate meaning and destiny.

Conclusion

The changing context demands the Christian community to take up the challenge to counter barriers and establish new partnership for witness within and outside the community to heal the wounds of people in the society. The enemies of the day for Northeast people particularly in the metro cities in India are racial discrimination, racial prejudices, ethnic division, disharmony, insensitivity for other and lack of qualitative faith life, etc. The sharing of the liberating message of Jesus and the warm hospitable nature of our people should lead to act against victimization, discrimination and perpetuation of evil practices in the society. They should be defeated within and outside the Christian community ultimately leading to the formation of a just and humane community in our midst.

Contributors

Rev. Dr. A. Temjen Jamir is the Associate Professor in the Department of Communication and the Academic Dean at the Clark Theological College, Mokokchung, Nagaland.

Ms. Achumlo Ezung is a teaching Faculty at Nagaland Bible College, Artang, Mokokchung, Nagaland.

Dr. Brightstar Jones Syiemlieh is the Principal of the John Roberts Theological Seminary, Shillong and an Associate Professor in the Department of New Testament.

Mr. Butesen Ozukum is the Communication Officer at NEICORD (North East India Committee on Relief and Development), Guwahati.

Dr. Eyingbeni Hümtsoe-Nienu teaches Christian Doctrine and Gender Theologies at Clark Theological College, Mokokchung, Nagaland.

Dr. Hukato N. Shohe is the Academic Dean at the Trinity Theological College, Dimapur, Nagaland.

Mr. Imtimenba Jamir is the Assistant Director at the Centre for Dalit/Subaltern Studies, New Delhi.

Rev. Dr. Prechard B. M. Basaiawmoit is a member of the Peace and Justice Committee, Presbyterian Churches of India, Shillong, Meghalaya.

Rev. Dr. Shimreingam L. Shimray is Professor and Head of the Department of Christian Ethics and Social Analysis at the Eastern Theological College, Jorhat, Assam.

Dr. Temjensosang is the Associate Professor and Head of the Department of Sociology at Nagaland University, Lumami, Nagaland.

Mr. Temsuyanger teaches Old Testament at the Clark Theological College, Mokokchung, Nagaland.

Mr. Toshi Aier teaches History of Christianity at the Clark Theological College, Mokokchung, Nagaland.